SAVING AMERICA'S

Grace

I look forward to disussing this more with you! Michelle

Rethinking Family Values,
Moral Politics, and the Culture War

MICHELLE DEEN

"Our lives begin to end the moment we become silent about things that matter."

Martin Luther King, Jr.

Dedicated to My Father

My favorite Republican who taught me
to stand in principle, for truth, with
courage—no matter the tide.

Acknowledgments

This book has been a long time in the making with various fits and starts, but always with the constant support of my family and friends. I appreciate all of you who never doubted that this book would come to fruition.

In particular, I'd like to thank my daughter, Alisa Deen, for her insightful feedback and editorial comments, and my editor, Donna Becch, whose words of wisdom were the final push that took this book from idea to reality.

I'd also like to thank Michael Hanrahan Publishing for their professional guidance and assistance in the various details involved in publishing this book, and Michael Bowker for generously sharing his wealth of knowledge and experience that spans every last aspect of producing a book, from writing to publishing and marketing.

Finally, I'd like to thank my colleagues Joyce Catlett and Robert Firestone, Ph.D. for writing the foreword and whose theoretical insights and our many discussions provided the seeds of thought from which this book took form.

First published in 2016 by Michelle Deen

ISBN: 978-0-9953572-4-2

Printed in the U.S. by Lightning Source
Project management and text design by Michael Hanrahan Publishing
Cover design by molly green graphic design (www.mollygreendesign.com)
Cover photo by Valerio Berdini (www.valerioberdini.com)

Extracts from *Goals for Americans: The Report of the President's
Commission on National Goals* used with permission from
The American Assembly, Columbia University

Contents

Foreword

Robert Firestone, Ph.D. and Joyce Catlett, M.A.

This well-argued, thoughtful book by Michelle Deen breaks through the almost impenetrable fog of slogans that for years has obscured the real meaning of family values. The book effectively deconstructs harmful societal precepts masquerading as ethical principles. For a generation, neoconservatives and the religious right have used the phrase "family values" as a truism or motto to advance their agenda. Sadly, many people have adopted these precepts as guidelines in an attempt to reclaim the romanticized "Father Knows Best" family of the 1950's—which they believe was all but destroyed by the "liberal establishment."

Saving America's Grace is especially timely in that it provides an in-depth scrutiny of issues that deeply concern Democrats and Republicans alike in the 2016 presidential election. As of this writing, major news channels and social media outlets are focusing considerable attention on the issues raised in this book.

For example, in *Salon.com,* Alex Henderson noted, "As the GOP presidential primary heats up and the 2016 election draws close, Republicans have been pandering to their far-right evangelical base and blaming social liberalism for the decline of 'family values' in the United States."[1]

The book traces the evolution, or to be more accurate, the devolution of modern conservatism after the Republican Party was infiltrated in the 1980's by the religious right who cleverly dubbed themselves the "Moral Majority." The author stresses the fact that this merger of political and religious forces breached the boundary between church and state established by our Constitution, precipitating an "authoritarian crusade to impose laws based on religious beliefs, which is another blatant disregard of America's founding principles."

Conservative leaders unabashedly continue to misuse the expression "traditional family values" to indoctrinate citizens with a set of beliefs, attitudes, and standards that are, in fact, diametrically opposed to authentic ethical principles based on humanism and the Golden Rule. As the author points out, the Golden Rule ("Do unto others as you would have them do unto you,") is a core moral principle "that lies not in religious dogma, but inside the soul, a quality of being no amount of legislation can instill, nurture or enforce." Her point of view reflects E.O. Wilson's stance on this issue, which he expressed in the following declaration, "I believe in the independence of moral values, whether from God or not, and I believe that moral values come from human beings alone, whether or not God exists."[2]

In her analysis of the nuclear family, the author points out significant differences between families where the members attempt to live by the Golden Rule and those based on the authoritarian model of obedience, patriarchy, and control. This level of analysis is crucial because it can uncover the deeper forces at work within the family, which if unexamined, cloud our awareness of and insight into faulty child-rearing practices in families that may need our help. In *The Ethics of Interpersonal Relationships* (2009) we (Robert Firestone and Joyce Catlett) emphasized the importance of this type of analysis: "An examination of the ethics of family life is vital because children are our heritage, the legacy we leave behind, and our hope for the future...This type of inquiry would lead to a painstaking examination of our priorities in relation to traditional family values." (p. 64)[3]

Authoritarian patriarchal families, as distinguished from more democratic authoritative families, tend to be characterized by flawed child-rearing practices that cannot be considered "ethical" in any sense of the word, because they fail to promote children's psychological and spiritual growth. In these families, "parents believe that to be properly socialized, children must be made to submit to parental authority 'for their own good.' ... They tend to equate discipline with punishment and feel justified in using harsh, forceful measures to enforce 'good' behavior" (Firestone & Catlett, 2009, p. 57).[4]

Many people fail to make a distinction between the images and rhetoric of traditional family values and the painful reality of everyday life in many families. Their arguments in support of "family values" are hypocritical and 180 degrees off course, that is, they confuse "the map with the territory."

Most people rely on shopworn explanations blaming social upheaval and personal suffering on the breakdown of religion and the dissolution of the family; however, the reverse is true. The deterioration in family relationships and social structure is largely a by-product of harmful practices within the family unit, rather than the result. (R.W. Firestone, 1997, p. 42).[5]

In later chapters, the author examines social and psychological factors underlying less-than-optimal child rearing practices that tend to be supported by "family values" rhetoric. She goes on to compare the nuclear family structure with that of an extended family, which existed for thousands of years before the nuclear family structure came into being.

We agree with her assertion that the extended family has many advantages over the nuclear family in relation to children's mental health and emotional well-being. And mounting scientific evidence tends to support our views as well as those of the author with respect to the benefits of an extended family network. In *Creating a Life of Meaning and Compassion*, we stated, "One of the major problems confronting the modern nuclear family is that its members are living isolated lives without the support network that was provided in past generations by the extended family... Human beings evolved not as individuals, but as communities or tribes, interdependent socially, emotionally and biologically." (p. 306).[6]

Despite its concern with political issues that tend to polarize people, *Saving America's Grace* is *not* a political rant, diatribe or polemic *against* the Republican Party, the religious right or conservatives as a whole. It's an informative and reader-friendly revelation of a cleverly disguised, biased viewpoint, which has contributed to the current Congressional gridlock.

Just as Laura Kipnis' popular book *Against Love: A Polemic* was not *really* a polemic *against* love, but an unveiling of the myriad images, roles and implicit restrictive rules of "coupledom," so, too, *Saving America's Grace* is an exposé of the mendacity and fabrication underlying family values rhetoric.

In her Introduction, the author states her purpose for writing this book: "*to provide the moral story that underlies the progressive vision,* a cause that has yet to be told but exists for many on an intuitive level. Progressives know what it takes to promote a sound society infused with the kind of character and grace that supports democracy in all its glory. They just don't know they know it."

Progressives *do* need to make their moral story more explicit and they need to promote it as persistently and as passionately as Republicans have done. The important question is, will they be able to accomplish this goal? Will they be able to persuade others to join them? Admittedly, it is difficult to change deeply held beliefs, internalized racism, and xenophobia in one generation. However, it is possible to approach these social and psychological problems with hope or at least cautious optimism.

The title of this book, *Saving America's Grace*, is reminiscent of another "moral story" recounted by former slave trader John Newton, who in 1779 wrote the words to the popular hymn, "Amazing Grace," and later the pamphlet, "Thoughts upon the Slave Trade." After converting to Christianity, Newton felt his eyes had been opened and he viewed life and people from a completely new perspective. In the pamphlet, he confesses, "It will always be a subject of humiliating reflection to me, that I was once an active instrument in a business that which my heart now shudders."

Newton's pamphlet was disseminated to every member of the British Parliament where it came to the attention of MP William Wilberforce. For the next two decades, Wilberforce brought the matter of the slave trade before Parliament where it was repeatedly voted down. Finally in 1807, Parliament passed the *Slave Trade Act*, which prohibited the buying and selling of human beings as property. In 1833, all slaves within the British Empire were granted their freedom.[7]

This historic event proves that people's core beliefs, worldviews, and even internalized prejudices can be changed. Prior to the passage of the *Slave Trade Act*, everyone matter-of-factly accepted the slave trade as a part of an essential commercial exchange between nations; they didn't *see* black people as members of the human race. Basically, after 1807, British subjects began to perceive the world through different eyes. In the words of the hymn, they "once were lost, but now they're found, were blind, but now they see."

Perhaps *Saving America's Grace*, like John Newton's pamphlet, will add fuel to the new progressive movement, which is already attracting increasing numbers of millennials (and other age groups), largely due to the influence of Bernie Sanders. Hopefully, progressives will embrace their own moral narrative and enter into civilized debate with conservatives to define the true meaning of family values. Who knows? We may once again be witness to an exciting sea change in people's basic perceptions and core beliefs, similar to what occurred in 1807.

We're seeing an exciting beginning. Let's hope this progressive movement continues to gain momentum.

Robert W. Firestone, Ph.D., author of *The Fantasy Bond* and *Overcoming the Destructive Inner Voice: True Stories of Therapy and Transformation* (forthcoming from Prometheus Books)

Joyce Catlett, M.A. co-author of *The Ethics of Interpersonal Relationships*

Preface

I consider myself an accidental activist.

Not that long ago my world of concern was fairly small: my family, my friends, my community, my clients, and my practice as a marriage and family therapist. I wasn't political. I didn't even vote. I had always been drawn to the more personal, intimate aspects of life, and had no use for the impersonal nature of government and big bureaucracies.

Then 9/11 hit.

I woke up, literally and figuratively, when my husband walked into our bedroom at six o'clock in the morning and said, "We've been attacked." I bolted upright, instantly awake but disoriented. I could feel the intensity and immensity of whatever was happening, but still wasn't clear what it was. He turned on the television and stunned disbelief paralyzed me as I watched the savagery and destruction unfold.

Suddenly, everything was different. This was not just a great tragedy; it was a capsizing event of profound proportions. The tidal wave of pain and fear that rolled across our country knocked a grim reality into my soul with a force that would never leave me, or my outlook, the same.

No more blissful ignorance. I had a new understanding of the value of freedom and security as never before. Like the rest of America, I was now concerned with the safety of the world, our children's world. Would my daughter be safe? Could I shelter her four-year-old eyes from the horror repeatedly displayed on televisions everywhere? Could I insulate her from the anxiety and panic of the adults around her whom she needed to feel secure? Would I ever be able to watch her play with light-hearted joy with the ever-present threat of evil appearing out of the blue on any given day?

Just as suddenly, my naïve worldview was flipped upside down. I understood that America in the eyes of others was not as I had imagined. My blind assumption that our government would always "do right" had me believing that all was well on the global-relations front. It was only when the debris from the twin towers swirled through Manhattan that I realized just how much America was despised by a vengeful, if small, segment of the world for reasons that are still, to this day, largely left untold in any depth by the media.

While these reasons could never justify the actions taken against us, or anyone anywhere in the world, it was crucial information to know and it enraged me that we'd been kept in the dark and lied to for the sake of expedience.

Then, when it was revealed that a fabricated story about "weapons of mass destruction" had been used as justification to wage war in Iraq, I was beside myself with fury. The moral corruption behind such an unjust war depicted an America I did not want to be a part of. While I'm not an expert on the geopolitical and ethnic complexities of the Middle East, common sense and human decency does tell me a thing or two about honorable vs. dishonorable courses of action. Using a false premise to invade a country, the deceit of the American public, and the war itself were all dishonorable actions, intolerable to me. Over 150,000 innocent children and civilians have been killed, which is never justifiable, let alone in a war that should never have been waged.

The wrong-headed march into an immoral war awakened in me an outrage at our political system, the likes of which I had never known. Something was horribly wrong in this democratic paradise of ours and I wanted to know more. I voraciously consumed news on politics and current events from both domestic and international sources, obsessed with what was happening in our nation's corridors of power.

Then the 2004 election hit me like a punch in the gut. I was sickened to the core that G.W. Bush had been re-elected President of the United States in spite of his grievous war actions. Once again, lies and half-truths, this time coming from his campaign operatives, had swayed our country away from moral truths, political integrity, and any hope of security, justice or peace in the near term.

Exactly how President Bush managed to get re-elected was a travesty that weighed on me. He slid into his second term in office by way of deceptive family values rhetoric, using same-sex marriage as a wedge issue. This rhetoric painted Republicans as moral heroes fighting a culture war to protect children and families from their newest propagandized weapons of mass destruction—gay people who wanted to marry. According to them, if marriage equality were to pass, family values would be destroyed, families would disintegrate, and civilized society would collapse. This artful deceit was unabashedly peddled to great effect, duping citizens and swinging middle of the road "values voters" to the ever-so-wrong Right.

That was it for me. No more. Not on my watch. Family relations was my area of expertise and I'd be damned if scheming politicians were going to use misinformation about family life to further their self-serving goals.

While I'm as straight as the hair on my head, I was not going to silently stand by while gay people were being used as scapegoats. Nor was I going to silently stand by when the so-called "family values advocates" of the religious right were hoodwinking families everywhere. Promoting myths and misinformation about what makes family life healthy does nothing to help families. In fact, it contributes to the very problems they claim to have the solutions for.

I started to write furiously in the middle of Bush's second term when a debilitating illness struck and sidelined me—for years. I watched the 2008 presidential race from a hospital bed and struggled to stay alive during Obama's first term in office. I had tucked the beginnings of this book away and watched as gay marriage rights picked up steam. I celebrated when marriage equality became law in 2015, and thought the need for the book I had started to write so long ago had passed.

Then with the presidential campaign of 2016, my outrage at the lack of moral character in politics was once again fired up. Led by Donald Trump, the Republican field of candidates stooped to lows never before seen in potential leaders of the free world. Unscrupulous behavior defined a campaign that became a free for all. The Republican Party had hopelessly lost control of their carefully crafted moral values messaging to Trump's outlandish remarks that had the media all over him like flies on cow dung. No longer could Republicans claim title to superior moral values. No how. No way.

The time was now for Democrats to take charge of a moral values platform. Although family values rhetoric has fallen by the wayside this election cycle after decades of strategic use, the need for a moral narrative to address the real problems of the nation was as great as ever. I began to write again. The result is this book.

This is a critical time in our country that calls for all of us to reconnect as a nation with what really matters. When everything else is stripped away—money, materialism, ego, vanity, and thirst for power—what is left is our humanity, our care and feeling for the plight and well-being of each other. Our grace.

Certain things in life change us in profound ways, making us acutely aware of what really matters. For me, becoming a mother and grappling with a life-threatening illness were catalysts. With motherhood, it became impossible to not feel the preciousness of children everywhere, and the absolute, indescribable, excruciating anguish of any parent having to witness their child suffering through a war—let alone maimed or killed in one. With my illness, I realized that life is short and that, when you have the capacity to do something you believe in, you must do it because that chance may not be there tomorrow.

Immediately after 9/11, we all became acutely aware of what really mattered. We were connected to each other. We had compassion for people we didn't even know and a desire to extend ourselves to help those in need. We heard stories of people risking their lives to save strangers, and of people literally giving the shirts off their backs to the lost and injured. In my own practice, married couples that before had only argued and complained about who took the trash out, embraced their vulnerability and declared how much they loved and appreciated each other. When awareness of the fragility of life was at the fore, everything else fell away and what was left was the essence of life—love, care and concern. This was the silver lining of that dark, dark day. It now serves as an example of America at its best.

We need not wait for another catastrophe to experience that deep sense of connection and mutual support again. What we need is a return to a higher standard, where moral politics and family values are firmly founded on quality of character, where Americans are known for the care with which we treat others and our own. By restoring these traits that once made our country great, we can save America's grace.

I hope you will join me in championing a better America.

INTRODUCTION

Saving America's Grace

Rethinking Family Values, Moral Politics and the Culture War

"Unless we reach deep inside to the values,
the spirit, the soul and the truth of human nature,
none of the other things we seek to do will ever
take us where we need to go."

Bill Clinton

T he time is ripe to begin viewing family values, morality and
the "culture war" in a different light. A progressive light. For
far too long, Republicans have unfittingly claimed the mantle of
moral superiority, out to fight the wrongs in our culture they claim
are perpetrated by "liberal values." Like a deer in the headlights,
Democrats have not known how to respond. This book offers that
response.

There is not a better time for progressives to step onto their moral platform in a big, bold way, replacing conservative's questionable mores and regressive patriarchal family values with their own principled vision. While Republicans have played the moral values card to their advantage—framing the debate, claiming the issues, and positioning themselves as morally superior to their liberal opponents—Democrats have shied away from addressing moral and spiritual issues, neither repudiating Republicans' purported moral authority, nor articulating their own. Silence has not served them well.

As cognitive linguist George Lakoff, renowned author and leading expert on moral values framing in politics has explained, voters vote according to their values—not facts, not reason, not policy proposals. What matters to people—their values, beliefs and attitudes—drives politics. Because of this, Lakoff has advised the Democratic Party to identify their values and communicate them loudly and proudly in order to connect with voters on the gut level of personal meaning. Without this, candidates are toast.

Many political analysts concluded that Senator John Kerry lost to the immensely unpopular George W. Bush in 2004 for this very reason—a failure to resonate with voters on the level of personal values. His stiff, fact-based approach, coupled with an onslaught of television ads challenging his moral character as a swift-boat pilot in Vietnam, cost him the election. Kerry, a bona fide war hero, was attacked on manufactured moral issues, knocked back on his heels into a defensive position, never to recover. Bullets carrying moral gunpowder almost always have the power to deliver a lethal blow especially if there's no resonance between candidate and constituency on the level of values.

Currently, Hillary Clinton is running the risk of making the very same mistakes as Kerry, and as she did in 2008—leading with her cerebral cortex, offering good reason after good reason why she is the candidate to elect. And all the while, she's speaking from a defensive fighting position as her moral authority is challenged—Benghazi, email servers, big donor dealings, her cozy relationship with Wall Street, extravagant speaking fees paid to her by corporate banks, etc. You name it; she's fighting it. In sports and politics, playing defense never scores you points or wins you games and elections. It's time for a little offense.

Now imagine if Hillary, or any candidate, came out of the gate, speaking from a place of *moral authority* expressing who she is by what she believes, and why she does what she does. When "vote for me" instead becomes "vote for the cause," the power of purpose takes over. When communicating the "why" is so principled the tone immediately shifts from opposition to mission. When the fight is based on, and for, a set of values, there is no repudiation. They are your values. End of debate. You're either with the candidate, or you're not.

By articulating the values underlying the progressive cause, a candidate's stands can resonate far and wide. The people who don't get it, never will. They are not your voters. The people who do get it, will really get it, and will be in rallying mode. And then there will be those "on the fencers" who come to understand the positions in a new way, a way that resonates with them on a deeper level than facts or policy proposals ever could. From here comes the fire of inspiration—to care, to vote, to fight for what's right.

This is what Bernie Sanders has done throughout the 2016 campaign—speaking to the heart, from the heart. While he hasn't directly articulated an overarching moral story, he's been fighting for moral principles—hard and true, piece-by-piece. His whole being has been in the game. His conviction is visceral; you can feel it. And the Left, particularly the young Left, is enthusiastically responding to his resonant message in impressive numbers, in spite of the fact there is a generation gap gigabytes wide.

This brings me to *the ultimate purpose of this book, to provide the moral story that underlies the progressive vision*, a cause that has yet to be told but exists for many on an intuitive level. Progressives know what it takes to promote a sound society infused with the kind of character and grace that supports democracy in all its glory. They just don't know they know it.

It's a story that once told, will offer those with progressive sensibilities a way of taking charge of moral values rhetoric, grounding their principles and serving as the basis for strong stands that resonate far and wide. It's a story that will allow Democrats to provide an eloquent and moving expression of their profound beliefs, heretofore chided by conservatives. No longer will progressives have to defend themselves from the righteous indignation of conservative pundits who derisively accuse liberals of being amoral, or in their more generous moments, "morally relativistic"—a loosey-goosey bunch guided by hedonistic whims and base impulses.

This is a story for people who crave a voice rooted in sound moral reasoning that rises above the fray of family values rhetoric. For people who care about their families and family life in general. For families who fit the conventional mold, and for those that don't. It's a story about family values that go deeper than superficial structure and traditional roles. For families whose greatest

4

desire is to teach their children to be good, decent people whose very presence strengthens society and enhances humankind.

This is a story about morals that go deeper than literal interpretations of holy books written thousands of years ago by the fallible hand of man, undergoing numerous translations hence. It's a story for those who know they are good, moral people yet do not subscribe to fundamentalist dogma—religious progressives of any and all beliefs, as well as agnostics, atheists, secularists, humanists, or whatever label you choose.

It's a story about democratic principles that are the foundation of America, a country whose truest tradition is the belief in the moral rightness of individual freedom derived from a humanistic faith in the inherent goodness of individuals—their unlimited potential, capacity for self-governance and commitment to the common good.

It's a story about a moral absolute that is nothing more and nothing less than the secularly sympathetic and doctrinally ubiquitous Golden Rule, a moral coordinate that lies not in religious dogma, but inside the soul, a quality of being no amount of legislation can instill, nurture or enforce. It's a story about empathy and compassion, the unifying transcendent traits of the human heart that usher in grace, allowing a healing force in our society to emerge.

The 2016 presidential campaign is a pivotal point in American politics, and has created an opportune time for Democrats to take control of the moral values narrative that no longer belongs to Republicans for reasons that have become frightfully obvious. They've had the spiritually vacuous, infinitely vulgar and despotic Donald Trump take the lead as their presidential nominee. Next, the Republicans' story of moral superiority has been challenged by Pope Francis and most of the Western world who have asserted that social and global responsibility (not the Republican Party's interest) are moral issues of the highest order.

And finally, the Republicans' family values brand is unraveling, becoming increasingly irrelevant as shifting demographics bring millennials' forward thinking, open-minded attitudes and values onto center stage. It's been a strategy that has anchored Republicans for decades, yet has lost the *gravitas* it once had, especially now that marriage equality is here and our society has remained standing, contrary to all their fear-inducing rhetoric. On many levels, Republicans have been thrown off their game like never before—leaderless, out of tune, out of luck, and scrambling to figure out just what their message is, if indeed, they have one.

No more playing on their moral terms. In numerous ways today's Republican Party has been the best example of the worst elements our culture and politics have to offer. It's time for progressives to take charge of the moral values narrative by putting forth their vision, and setting the course for righting a culture and political system gone awry.

The place to begin is by speaking to the fears that the so-called "culture warriors" of the religious right have embedded in people's minds, Right and Left. We have to acknowledge what we know as true—that in many ways our culture *is* turning into a moral cesspool, and American families are in crisis. And contrary to their claims, all of us—liberals as well as conservatives, homosexuals as well as heterosexuals, religious and non-religious alike—value families. None of us want family life to become a relic of the past, although its form is changing, has always changed, and will continue to change.

In spite of all the partisanship, there is common ground among Americans across the aisle—the wish for sound families and well-adjusted children, for upstanding citizenship, for a more wholesome culture, and for most of us anyway, politics that actually serve the interests of the majority. In many ways, the Right and Left are not that far apart in their hopes for a more sound society. The biggest differences lie in beliefs about how to get there.

The Left has yet to articulate their view of the moral problems we face and their corresponding solutions, while the culture warriors on the Right have identified the wrong enemies and have been fighting the wrong war. If we step outside the box contrived by right-wing strategists and reframe the culture war itself, we'll find a fresh take on an old problem. We'll find something richer, deeper, and truer to coalesce around, pool our collective energies toward, and gradually rectify our society's spiritual abyss. When we do, we will find that the answers to our troubled society lie at the heart of the progressive cause.

As Reverend Jim Wallace, the author of *God's Politics* instructs, in order to appeal to those who care about moral values in politics, Democrats don't need to worry about moving left or moving center. The answer involves going deeper, laying out a moral values framework that speaks to many by grounding us in a common humanity. Only then can we move forward in creating a more perfect union, strengthening our society and country in ways that we haven't seen in partisan politics for far too long. From here, we just might be able to save America's grace.

1
A New Moral Story

"Remember: The most perfect machinery of government
will not keep us as a nation from destruction if there
is not within us a soul."

President Theodore Roosevelt

Emotions are roiling and the stakes are high as we sit perched on a grave tipping point in America today—a time when all is not well in the land of the free. Uncontrolled gun violence, extreme economic disparity, ongoing environmental degradation, unaffordable health care and college education, massive debt, deepening military entanglements in the Middle East, and mushrooming terrorism are momentous issues calling for the right responses, for the right reasons, with just the right touch. Each of these situations is so tenuous and consequences so dire that we need to have our moral sensibilities screwed on tight, with wisdom, keen judgment and good grace directing our actions like never before.

Yet, we're in the midst of an impassioned polarization of mores in our country that has hamstrung much of our political process and is threatening our foundation as a nation united by common principles. Of course, robust debate is inherent in a democracy, even beneficial. But the unscrupulous infighting between and within parties today is weakening America, sucking the soul out of a country that was once a model for the world—a beckoning light of freedom, goodwill and unbound opportunity. Now, America embodies a beaconing—a warning of what can go wrong when the moral precepts of democracy are degraded by runaway capitalism, egoistic concerns, and the unbound power of a covert ruling class. It's up to progressives to right such wrongs before these dangerous values take our country down.

Throughout the 2016 primary season, we've seen reprehensible behavior from the Republican Party—a party in utter meltdown, with no moral message, no sage leadership, and no refined respectability on display. Rather, disgraceful qualities of character have been running the show, a show as ridiculous as a *Three Stooges* skit. While this farce hasn't been funny and the slapstick not physical, the 2016 presidential campaign has been an exaggerated, improbable and absurd display of random attacks and counter-attacks by one-dimensional characters without depth or sophistication. We've had bullies on the playground throwing sand, not prospective leaders of the free world taking courageous stands for a better world.

And the biggest kicker: The more ignoble and shameful the behavior, the more favorable the candidate's ratings. Why should this be? How can we live in a society where a significant faction applauds treating others poorly? Where mindless, crass, selfish attitudes and values are exalted? What has happened to good grace being a moral standard? And what has happened to the wisdom of our moral heroes whose leadership was so integral to the story of America?

When it comes to disgraceful behavior marring America, right-wing punditry is no better. Indeed, it fans the flames of partisan fire. Aggressive, inciting rhetoric promoting xenophobia and misogyny is daily fare, while hostile treatment is leveled against anyone with a differing opinion. Shouting over and belittling guests reaps ratings, not intelligent discourse. Seething war language permeates everything; even plain red coffee cups evoke paranoia about a perceived war on Christmas and becomes headline news—for days. Strife, contempt and provocation ooze from our news media with abandon, providing cheap entertainment under the guise of need-to-know information.

In fact, punditry as a lowbrow slugfest has become so normal it doesn't even register as the pitiful behavior it is—an undignified display of cultural insensibility to which we have become anesthetized. And to top it all off, our children are absorbing these base behaviors as the norm, witnessing role models that have no business being in prominent positions. Our principles, purpose and ideas of success and leadership, which should unequivocally involve upstanding character, have become perverted beyond recognition. Unless we do something about it, America will become perverted beyond recognition.

We have a tragic problem here, a problem that cannot be pinned on the usual scapegoats of cultural crudity—liberalism and a secular society. This plight is far more fundamental. It involves a breakdown in character and common human decency, fostering a burgeoning disregard for each other—a lack of care, concern and connection, without which society severely suffers. And when it manifests in our country's leaders, we are in deep, deep trouble, having lost the moral bearings that are crucial for a functioning democracy. We are a society in danger of losing its soul.

We're up against a rudimentary partisan conflict that cuts to the core of who we are as people, and what is the right way to proceed in government, as in life. Do we operate from an altruistic place of compassion, empathy and concern for each other, using respectful debate, diplomacy, judiciousness, and humanitarian principles, or from an authoritarian place of fear, anger, cynicism and divisiveness, using power with callous disregard as a governing force?

As a society and as individuals, we're faced with the perennial challenge that philosophers and religious leaders have expounded upon over the world and over the ages. Do we choose love or fear? Do we turn to the light, or dwell in darkness? Do we seek unity or divisiveness? Do we embrace altruism or authoritarianism? It's hard to deny that love, unity and altruism are the more exalted elements of human nature— elements that a country like America, one based on principles intended to serve the highest potential of humankind, can and must embody. Otherwise, America will never be the best that she can be...or even the America she was intended to be.

At the Republican National Convention in 1992, Pat Buchanan gave a famous speech declaring that a cultural war for the soul of America was raging, a war critical to determining the kind of country we shall be. "My friends, this election is about much more than who gets what," Buchanan said. "It is about who we are." "Who we are" has never been more relevant than today. It is a good-vs.-evil battle to return to the altruistic moral underpinnings on which our democracy is based.

Fighting for the soul of America is precisely the mission Democrats need to take on—now—with zeal. The Republicans' authoritarian moral paradigm that is unabashedly anti-American has encroached so far into their party that the entire cast of presidential candidates has pushed fear, anger, cynicism and divisiveness to great effect. The more outrageous the demagoguery, the better the poll results.

Many prominent political commentators are acknowledging just how far off base the Republican Party has traveled. An article published on the website of esteemed journalist Bill Moyers reports that Peggy Noonan, speechwriter for Ronald Reagan, lamented on Super Tuesday: "We're seeing a great political party shatter before our eyes." The author of this article went on to describe the morphing of the GOP into an anti-American bundle of human vacuity. It states that we're witnessing "...the decades-long transformation of Republicanism from a business-centered, small town, white Protestant set of beliefs into quite possibly America's primary institutional force of bigotry, intellectual dishonesty, ignorance, warmongering, intractability and cruelty against the vulnerable and powerless."[8]

There's been an insidious creep of authoritarianism into the Republican Party over the decades, drastically changing the face of conservatism in America. John W. Dean, who served as legal counsel in the Nixon administration, explores this phenomenon in his book, *Conservatives Without Conscience*. In it, he explains that conservatism has historically been difficult to define, but it has essentially set out to "draw on the proven wisdom of the past, not debase the dignity of others, and maximize freedom consistent with necessary safety and order."[9] If we look at the campaign messages that have come out of the Republican Party, each of these rudiments of conservatism are betrayed. There has been an utter failure to honor our founders' noble intentions for American democracy—the moral tenets of liberty, equality and the common good.

Not only does today's Republican Party not hew to these core moral dictates, but they've also been on an authoritarian moral crusade to impose laws based on religious beliefs, which is another blatant disregard of America's founding principles. Dean notes that religious moralizing, and the authoritarianism that comes along with it, were never part of modern conservatism until the religious right began to infiltrate the Republican Party in the 1980's.[10] With the penetration of authoritarian values, attempts to restrict personal freedoms through the legislation of biblical beliefs became part and parcel of the Republican platform.

Due to the religious right's potent capacity for fundraising and the strength of their media and messaging machine, political conservatives of all stripes jumped into bed with religious activists, each taking advantage of the other's influence. Steeped in an authoritarian worldview, these religious fundamentalists-cum-political crusaders impregnated the Republican Party with their moral ideology. And with their large, passionate and influential following, the religious right has transformed and powered the base of the conservative cause.

It was this marriage of convenience that birthed the Republicans' family values brand. As they built their brand out with clever framing around wholesome, traditional family values and narratives of moral superiority, authoritarianism gradually became associated with American values. Then, when George W. Bush came out swinging after 9/11 with his morally righteous nationalism, authoritarian values became overtly (and wrongly) associated with American patriotism.

In the so-called War against Terrorism, Bush wielded a rogue cowboy act with great aplomb, declaring: "You're either with us or against us." Preying on heightened fears, he stirred up an "us vs. them" sentiment to justify war with the so-called "evildoers" in Iraq, a country that had nothing to do with the terrorist attacks. Republican candidates have been employing the same authoritarian fear-mongering strategy ever since. Using terrorist attacks as an opportunity to thump their chests, they've been posturing for an epic showdown with "Islamic terrorists" while demonizing and throwing all Muslims under the bus, the most un-American of values paraded with the most misplaced pride.

Without any qualms whatsoever, Republicans have used irresponsible rhetoric to curry favor for self-serving political purposes at the expense of our nation. By first stoking fear about "the evildoers," then positioning themselves as the destroyer of evil, candidates create superhero narratives featuring none other than themselves. These tactics may be advantageous for getting votes, but they are dreadfully ignorant, playing straight into the good guy/bad guy trap that the terrorists have set. The more America's political leaders become tyrannically unhinged with their blustery, aggressive, over-reactive theatrics, the more right the terrorists look to those they are trying to mobilize. In their effort to garner more votes from the right-wing base, Republican candidates are helping terrorists garner more recruits, not a move with America's best interests in mind.

Republican presidential candidate Donald Trump gained his early lead in the polls by employing this type of authoritarianism to the hilt—getting tough on Mexican immigrants (categorized by him as rapists and criminals) whom he would throw out on their ear, then build a concrete wall to keep them there. Because of his "crush-the-enemy, we-will-prevail" brand that he pulled off so well, Trump led the Republican presidential polls for months on end, in spite of the fact he had zero experience in politics, diplomacy, or government, and has become their 2016 presidential nominee.

Based on what we've seen from his disposition on the campaign trail, Trump's approach to handling the volatile circumstances in the Middle East would be akin to turning a lunatic loose on a hornet's nest, stick in hand. His *modus operandi* is to rile people up, and then play on their emotions—the more extreme the emotions and crazier the reactions, the better Trump likes it. Ted Cruz, Marco Rubio, and the rest of the Republican field who also flaunted authoritarianism and inspired "us vs. them" sentiments were no better. Employing this type of rhetoric is dangerous to the well-being of America.

This critical time calls for moral leadership of the utmost clarity, yet we're seeing an exceeding lack of moral intelligence among Republican presidential contenders, across the board, like never before. While authoritarianism appeals to those who believe moral order is obtained through obedience and submission to power, authoritarianism is *not* moral intelligence, and does not constitute favorable leadership skills.

In her book, *Building Moral Intelligence* (2006), Michele Borba identified seven key virtues that are critical components of moral intelligence, which also happen to correspond with excellence in leadership. They are: empathy, conscience, self-control, respect, kindness, tolerance and fairness.[11] As we can see, authoritarianism couldn't be more contrary to the components of moral intelligence outlined here, so much so that authoritarianism would be better described as a moral disability or handicap—the last thing we need in an American president today.

However, the attraction some have to authoritarian leadership is unmistakable, and isn't entirely irrational. It's important to understand the psychology beneath this worldview. Psychologist Bob Altemeyer from the University of Manitoba has done extensive research ferreting out the qualities inherent in authoritarian personalities, characteristics that explain the gravitation toward conservative ideology and religious fundamentalism. He's distinguished two types of authoritarian personalities—followers and leaders, who fit together like hand in glove.

Followers appear to be driven by a high degree of underlying fear and anxiety. Altemeyer found that followers need "constancy, familiarity, black and white rules, and are averse to change, 'otherness' or ambiguity."[12] They tend to have compartmentalized thinking and rigid beliefs combined with little self-awareness. Since the unfamiliar is threatening to them, we can see where the tendencies toward racism, xenophobia, and aggressiveness toward anyone who does not adhere to their particular belief system come from.

We can also see the draw to conservatism with its emphasis on stability and conformity to tradition, and to religious fundamentalism with its emphasis on biblical literalism where right and wrong is black and white. And as an extra bonus with religious fundamentalism, there's a powerful Father figure in the sky to tell them what to do (so they don't have to grapple with uncertainty) and to promise them life everlasting, a comforting thought.[13]

Having leaders who project power gives authoritarian followers a feeling of safety. Like a pack of dogs taking cues from the alpha male, they are ready to submit to commands to attack or act aggressively. But unlike our canine friends, authoritarian personalities tend to have submerged anger boiling away, searching for a release. According to Altemeyer, they are hostile people waiting for something to be hostile about, and authoritarian leaders are skillful at tapping into that drive to fuel their righteous cause.[14] This had been on full display at Trump rallies where racism, xenophobia and general aggression is stirred with ease and physical violence frequently erupts.

Altemeyer delineates two types of authoritarian leaders— those with a "social dominance orientation" and the "double highs," who carry the fear-based characteristics of followers with a socially dominant overlay. The double-highs are considered to be the most dangerous because their control involves the unsavory characteristics of social dominators along with the deeply rooted fear and fanaticism that followers possess. Those with a social dominance orientation are prejudicial, of course, given that a need to feel superior over others comes with dominance. And they have all the wicked characteristics you would expect from any cartoon villain—they are intimidating, ruthless, vengeful, unfeeling, and scorn noble acts like kindness and charity. Most of all, they are leaders because "They love power, including the power to hurt in their drive to the top."[15]

We're seeing all types of authoritarian characteristics among Republican candidates and their supporters today—a very basic and horrific lack of human empathy combined with righteous aggression. Reckless bravado has replaced measured wisdom and responsibility, gangster swagger has replaced dignified humility and sophistication, and throwing one's weight around has replaced civil discourse and diplomacy. Move over respectability. Extremism is the new normal. Deplorable is the new black.

As a result of this devolution in taste, grace and sensibility, America is at risk of losing even more respect on the world stage, and of being perceived as a soulless, greedy, bullying nation with only self-interest in mind. Without shrewd statesmanship that focuses on nation building rather than warmongering, and without a goal of unity and cooperation in solving problems inside and outside our country, we'll set ourselves up for an eye-for-an-eye mentality. Nothing good can come of this. I don't think any of us want our children to live with the prospect of having enemies around every corner. I certainly don't.

A massive change is necessary *now*, or we will be spiraling down a black hole of social and governmental depravity before we know it, not unlike some of the unsavory foreign regimes we attempt to school. If we truly want to "Make America Great Again," as in Donald Trump's seductive tagline, we need to start with respect and dignity and empathic concern for one another, within our borders and with the rest of our world. There is no other way. In fact, there is no other America.

The idea of American democracy has always been rooted in elevated moral principles, the likes of which had never before been realized in any government. In the 1830's, the French statesman Alexis de Tocqueville recognized that something extraordinary was unfolding in this land of liberty, thus made it his mission to observe and write about America. He concluded: "America is great because she is good, and if America ever ceases to be good, America will cease to be great."[16]

Unlike Trump, de Tocqueville understood that American democracy relies on a high level of human conscience in order to self-govern (and, I would add, keep the heady tendencies of military, economic, and political power in check). What we need is not authoritarianism, but conscientious compassion and dedication to the well-being of all—united we stand, divided we fall. Virtue is at the very core of America's greatness. Without it, the finest intentions of our democracy fall apart.

The National Center for Constitutional Studies confirms this point of view, stating on their website that the more "thoughtful citizens have seen society as primarily moral in origin: a community of souls."[17] Indeed, forming a more perfect *union* is the moral law on which the Constitution is based. Unfortunately, to the detriment of our country, divisiveness, not unity, has been fueling politics of late. With the right-wing media that simultaneously feeds off anger and fear while feeding anger and fear, we have a vortex of hate-mongering swirling round and round, sucking us down to the lowest versions of ourselves, not unlike waste down a toilet.

Our dressed-as-news entertainment is powerful entrainment that yields positive ratings that yield dollars and cents. It's a supremely influential industry that turns shouting heads into celebrities with zealous followers, frenzies the right-wing base, and dominates political discourse across the nation. These shock-jock media mavens like Rush Limbaugh, Ann Coulter, and Bill O'Reilly know how to work their audience like putty in the palm of their hands, manipulating emotions and sculpting conservative viewpoints while using bluster and blow to drown out any possibility of logic or reason.

The authoritarian attitudes and viewpoints peddled by right-wing media, then amplified through social media, have pushed these beliefs into mainstream, changing the face of the Republican Party. Establishment Republicans now reflect the extreme views of its base—hostile to the values that make America, America. In truth, Republicans are *not* the party of superior morality. They're a party in absolute betrayal of America's values and mores. They are a party that has lost its soul.

Let's take a look at their story of moral superiority successfully touted, yet inherently and fatally flawed—a story that we can finally put to rest.

Republicans, Family Values, and the Mendacity of Moral Superiority

In addition to the dishonorable qualities of character coloring the Republican Party, their long-standing corner on the morality market is slipping away for another reason entirely. Their family values brand is losing its lusty appeal. With shifting demographics and attitudes, along with the recent Supreme Court ruling in favor of marriage equality, the Right has lost their main rhetorical tactic—inducing fear that same-sex marriage will harm society (there's that use of fear and divisiveness again)—that had voters charging to the polls. But alas, marriage equality is here. Society has not been destroyed. Ho-hum has replaced panic across the land. And the fight for traditional family values does not have the punch or sway of moral righteousness it once had.

Since the ruling, which effectively capped the Republicans' decades-long family values strategy, the religious right has been scrambling to rebrand their culture war from a "fight for traditional family values" to a "fight for religious liberty." Same goal, different packaging. Ultimately, their unspoken aim, as it's always been, is to turn fundamentalist biblical beliefs into law, tampering with democracy and all kinds of civil rights, personal liberties and science-based facts that go along with it: Abortion. Contraception. Gay marriage. Sex education. The teaching of evolution in schools, etc.

The religious right's particular view of morality is so narrow and their preoccupation with sex so all-consuming that the focus rarely leaves the genitals to areas of real human concern like poverty, homelessness, health care and childcare, mass shootings, war and humane immigration policies. These are the types of issues a democratic government is designed to address—social and humanitarian issues—not personal or religious issues. When politicians believe access to birth control is more concerning than access to guns, when there's more concern among politicians about what people do in the privacy of their bedroom than about the cold and hungry people on the street, something is seriously amiss.

What's missing is soul.

True Christians are driven by compassion and would ordinarily be compelled by these human concerns—if they weren't blinded by ideology hollowing out the soul. Yet, these are the types of problems that "amoral liberals" are determined to alleviate, as they push for laws supporting basic human rights and liberties. Progressives, promoting true democratic principles from a place of empathy, compassion and altruism, certainly do have a moral leg to stand on. It's time to assert it.

Witnessing the current state of moral disorientation in American government, Pope Francis stepped straight into the crossfire of the culture war when addressing the U.S. Congress during his 2015 visit. He admonished our public servants to rethink our values, to pursue social justice causes first and foremost, to be stewards of the environment, and to govern with the goal of enhancing the common good. In short, he urged our politicians to put humanistic values before capitalistic values, an indictment of a culture that worships money at the expense of human cause, concern and common decency.

This threw conservatives into a tizzy, showing the somewhat amusing audacity to criticize the Pope's wisdom. They complained that the Pope should not speak to global warming because he's not a scientist, nor economics because he's not an economist, and should stick to his business: religion and morality.

This is the gross error in the Republican mindset. The very fact that conservative ideologues cannot see that economic and environmental policies *have moral implications and should be grounded in moral principles* is precisely the problem and the gist of Pope Francis' address. He was emphasizing that these are moral matters that call for moral responses. He wisely pointed out that the love of money should never override the love of humanity and reminded us that we have a moral obligation to take care of each other, including the earth, our shared environment. His message was simple. His message was profound. His message was the Golden Rule.

It's time to rethink morality in our ever-evolving democracy, and take moral standards back from those who narrowly equate morality with authoritarian principles and sexual repression. It's time to remind ourselves that capitalism and its counterpart, consumerism, is never more important than the well-being of others. It's time to get money out of politics in order to diminish corruption and self-serving interests chipping away at the common good. It's time to claim the Golden Rule as our guiding principle.

It's time to understand morality in a broader light that encompasses quality of character and how we treat one another. This requires empathy and compassion, with or without religion. An anonymous quote says it best: "You don't need religion to have morals. If you can't determine right from wrong, you lack empathy not religion." Spot on. Just ask Josh Duggar, or take a look around. There are plenty of examples to be found.

It's time to turn the tables on the Republican narrative of moral superiority and reclaim the virtues that make America, America. If our goal is to create a better America, it has to start with sound character—of our leaders on both sides of the aisle who serve to guide us, of citizens who create our society, and of parents who are molding our children and through them, the future. And yes, family values are paramount, but not the type the religious right proclaims. While most of us can agree that families are the building blocks of society and are crucial for nurturing the emotional, spiritual and moral development of children, traditional family values (code for authoritarian, patriarchal, biblical values) are not the answer, as I will show in the chapters to follow.

In order to begin the task of reassessing our moral compass, we'll take a good hard look at traditional family values and associated rhetoric, where it all began for the Republican brand. Once the fantastical rhetoric is deconstructed, we'll reframe family values, and set the record straight on what it really takes to create happy homes, healthy souls and well-adjusted children. We'll find that the answer to a better America does not lie in a never-ending culture war, fighting to turn our democracy into a quasi-theocracy. The answer lies in a *cultural evolution* where sound character emerges through personal and spiritual development, bringing soulfulness and grace into American culture and politics. The strength of our country depends on it.

2

Family Values Rhetoric and the Duping of America

"Our major obligation is not to mistake
slogans for solutions."

Edward R. Murrow

O ver the decades, we've come to associate the Republican
Party with family values, the party to turn to when families,
children, and the coarsening of our culture is a primary concern.
This brilliant brand positioning has served to capture attention,
enamor voters and seal the deal at the polls for Republicans time
and again. The 2016 election cycle is the first time since the Reagan years that family values rhetoric hasn't taken center stage,
likely due to Trump hijacking the campaign with his unique
brand of nuttery, and the petering outrage over gay marriage. Yet,

in order to understand the persuasive power and problems with the Republican moral narrative and offer an alternative, family values rhetoric is the place to begin.

The phrase "family values" has been a supremely effective campaign slogan because it manages to dig right in, hitting the core of constituents' concerns, red and blue. It's been the political packaging tool of our time, a rhetorical device so sublime it bypasses the rational, analytical centers of the brain and goes straight to the heart of what matters to most—without getting to the heart of any matter at all.

It *just* resonates.

And therein lies its power. It grabs the soul and doesn't let go.

Intuitively, we all seem to know that the family in which we are raised profoundly influences whom we become. We know it in our gut, where our earliest experiences and brightest and darkest memories bring meaning into our lives. From this internal data bank, we derive a sense of who we are, what drives the choices we make, and whose voice we hear when confronted with life's challenges. We know that something gets passed along, a mysterious channeling of feelings, attitudes and beliefs that imbue the soul as surely as parents' genetic material infuses the cells of offspring.

Throughout this book, we'll uncover the mystery of this *something*, what I will refer to as *family values of real value*, the qualities within family relationships that promote solid character, moral integrity and the capacity for healthy relationships, responsible citizenry, and ultimately a sound society. We'll find that family values of real value are quite distinct from the ideology trumpeted by social and religious conservatives, shallow values that focus on proper form, traditional roles and obedience to dogma. In fact, in many ways family values of real *value* are in direct contrast to traditional family values: A patriarchal, authoritarian ideology based on control and submission that has little to do with inherent human needs, compromising family life and optimum human development in the process.

The first order of business is to decipher the family values rhetoric that's been fed to us, to see the trickery behind its use and understand how this something has been turned into something it's not. We'll come to see how the term "family values" has been bastardized, stripped of real meaning through misuse and overuse. How raw, intuitive truth has been usurped by manufactured messages used for political purposes. How false ideals have been promoted for an agenda that is mostly hidden from view, an agenda that may be well intended but is tragically off the mark. And we'll come to see how we've been banging around inside a box of flawed assumptions, trapped in a classic paradox wherein the so-called solutions are actually part of the problem.

While the conservatives' shrewd family values marketing strategy has worked for the better part of the last thirty-plus years, swinging middle of the road "values voters" to the right time and again, it will lose much of its power (and potential for damage) once we deconstruct the myths and misconceptions that have propped up this moral values framework.

As with any web of distortions, in between the knotty twists and turns, there are many holes to be found. I will point these out while redefining family values based on principles of human development and family relations, and show how the very principles that create strong families, moral children and a spiritually sound society lie at the heart of the progressive cause.

K Street Meets Madison Avenue

In the 1970's, right-wing think tanks organized and hunkered down, determined to generate a counter-revolution to derail the 60's surge of civil rights causes and progressive activism. What this cunning crew figured out was that the game of electoral politics, like the world of selling consumer goods, could be won with superior marketing techniques.

Following the gospel of Madison Avenue, they found their strategy: first you tap into a desire or concoct a need through emotional channels of longing, insecurity and fear, and then you *claim* to meet that need. This becomes your story, your brand, your identity. It doesn't matter if the story is complete nonsense. If told often enough, hogwash turns into brainwash and the contrived story becomes real. Next, you sell your brand with slogans and symbols that associate the product (or in this case party, candidate, platform) with the essence of your story in as few words as possible. Bam! Bam! Bam! A new reality is hammered home.

The Moral Majority. Pro-family. Pro-life. Family values. Values voters. Compassionate conservatives. Any way these sound bites are sliced, right-wing ideologues cornered the market on our most precious concerns—from those that tug on the heartstrings of our most intimate affairs, to the sweeping ideals of sound democracies. And in doing so, they built a brand identity that was hard to beat.

In many ways it makes sense that moral values language is a high-octane technique for packaging political parties and candidates. Moral paradigms (in principle, at least) are always at the heart of politics, defining, guiding and providing a meaningful context for political positions, decisions and movements, just as values and moral beliefs served as our country's raison d'être. And in no uncertain terms, voters elect representatives, politicians who most closely represent what they care about, believe in, stand for, and want to see realized in society. It's all about personal meaning, identity, and identifying with candidates emotionally and philosophically.

But things become more complex when slick rhetoric is added into the mix. The nonstop wash of values rhetoric has alternatively seduced and confused us, establishing a not-so-wise conventional wisdom that we've swallowed whole, without question. To borrow the famous term coined by satirical news commentator Stephen Colbert, we've been submerged in a "truthiness" that has been given far too little thought. Then George Lakoff came onto the scene with his book, *Don't Think of An Elephant: Know Your Values and Frame the Debate*, a handbook that grew from his more theoretical literary endeavor, *Moral Politics*.

Lakoff, a UC Berkeley cognitive linguist turned political framing expert, astutely nailed the underlying structure of right-wing rhetoric as the family values frame, an effectively grand, overarching strategy. Who doesn't care about family, and thereby, have family values? Is there anything that can penetrate the heart as profoundly? That speaks to personal history, immediate concerns, future hopes and fears in one fell swoop? The power of family values rhetoric is so engaging that it has captured an entire spectrum of voters from suburban soccer moms to rural gun-toters, and has brought together the most unlikely Republican bedfellows—theocons, neocons, libertarians, and anything in between—all willing to wave the family values flag to win the favor of voters.

And win it has, so masterfully that family values framing has been described as "an undeniably potent right-wing strategy: the effort to paint Dems as anti-family."[18] Just how potent was this strategy? According to a study published by the Progressive Policy Institute:

> *"Pro-family rhetoric has been responsible for (Democrats) losing married parents with young children in droves, that's 28% of the electorate translating into 33.6 million voters. During the last two presidential elections, the growing 'parent gap' became dramatically apparent with Al Gore losing married parents to George W. Bush by 15% points, and with John Kerry widening the gap, losing them by a whopping 19 points, 59–40. And here's the real kicker...most of these married parents with kids don't consider themselves conservative. Of this population, 45% were self-identified moderates and 16% identify themselves as liberals."[19]*

How can this be?

Underlying the family values brand is a story that portrays Republicans as heroes in a culture war against liberals whose amoral ways will hurt children and families. It's a narrative that hooks and holds, right down to the formulation of good guys and bad guys. Which side voters should take has been written into the script.

Gotcha, Dems! You've been framed.

The study explained this shift to the right as life-stage conservatism, rooted in parental responsibility to teach children right from wrong. In the 2004 exit polls voters were asked to name the one issue that mattered most in their presidential voting decision and 27% of married parents chose moral values—as opposed to 20% of the rest of the electorate. The author of this article concluded that Democrats would not win parents back until they took sides in the fight against a corrosive popular culture.

In truth, liberals as well as conservatives care about protecting children and families. We all have a vested interest in changing the coarse nature of our society. The unrelenting violence, soulless media, premature sexualization of children in advertising, rampant consumerism, mindless celebrity worship, drug use, and promiscuity in the way-too-young are problems for any American with any shred of sense. The difference is that Democrats have avoided addressing these issues because they don't know how. They have conceded this critical territory to the bellicose religious right and their party sycophants, losing out on a rich opportunity to meaningfully connect on a values level with voters.

Democrats can step into the game and compete for the heart of values voters instead of watching from the sidelines as Republicans run with the ball. By framing cultural and political problems in a different light, Democrats can show how progressive values are not the root of such problems, nor are they anti-American; they are the solution, true to America's core values. As these chapters unfold, this is precisely what we will do.

Family Values and the Culture War

Family values and the culture war are tightly intertwined concepts. The culture warriors' purported mission is to save our country, families and children from moral decay. How, pray tell? With legislation enforcing traditional family values (code for fundamentalist biblical beliefs), effectively turning America into a quasi-theocracy.

Fighting this culture war is an army of affiliated councils, associations, and institutes all carrying official sounding names usually with the words "family" or "values," mixed in, milking these terms for all they're worth. These agenda-driven organizations are heavily funded to the tune of hundreds of millions of dollars *per year*, employing partisan strategists, lawyers, and lobbyists with rigid ideologies to drive, speaking *as if* they have the requisite authority in family studies. They don't. They've merely packaged themselves that way, dubbing themselves "family values advocates."

Ironically, the patriarchal family values these ideologically driven advocates espouse are actually *contrary* to what experts in the field have found to benefit families. What we have here are wolves in sheep's clothing. Granted, some of these wolves may think they are sheep, with no intention of deception. Yet, this doesn't make their falsehoods truth, or misguided mission noble. The bottom line deception brought about by family values rhetoric is tragically harmful for our society, hindering our ability to actually help families and redirect a culture gone awry. By stripping away the rhetoric, we can see what this so-called war is really all about: the staunch march toward Christian fundamentalism wrapped in a package of family values rhetoric.

War a-Drummin' and a-Spinnin'

The battle cry to return America to a land of traditional family values rang most notably with Dan Quayle's clumsy attempt in the early '90s to publicly scold TV sitcom character Murphy Brown for proudly choosing single motherhood. He caused quite a stir, alternatively applauded and scoffed at by pundits and journalists. Over time it became clear that Americans were, (in practice anyway) turning a deaf ear, ignoring the rants and many of the values the right wing proclaimed sacred.

As Gerald Celente, founder of the Trends Research Institute noted:

> "...their [the religious right's] moral crusade to legislate lost family values back into mainstream America was as futile as legislation designed to bring back the horse and carriage would have been."[20]

When their battle cry didn't work, it was time for an all-out culture war. So they brought in the war drums, working voters into a feverish lather by casting liberal politicians as an anti-American, anti-family force that must be stopped.

Borrowing from the neocon's favorite playbook, these religious activists knew that by creating divisions of good vs. evil within the context of fear, they could create a loyal following. And, what is it that we most want to protect? Our children and families, of course. So straight to the heart they went, injecting the public with fear about family life and the well-being of our children.

Examples of their fear-inducing rhetoric hid in plain sight on the *Focus on the Family Action* website whose tagline was (predictably) "informing, inspiring and rallying those who care deeply about the family..." Here is one of many examples of their unabashed attempts to manipulate through fear:

"For really 40 years I have been watching a nonstop withering attack from social and political liberals that is tearing family apart, undermining marriage, belittling Christian values and endangering our children."[21]

Can you taste the fear?

To lessen the chance that their extremism would alienate moderates, they used wedge issues to gather broad support. In the early 2000's, their greatest leverage was the supposed protection of families by opposing gay marriage rights. In an article from their political action e-zine, *CitizenLink*, "What's the Big Deal about Gay Marriage?" James Dobson, founder of Focus on the Family, states:

"The seismic waves from same-sex marriage and parenting have the potential to deconstruct humanity."[22]

Translation: we are faced with rampant evil forces and better turn to Daddy Dobson and his ilk for protection from cataclysmic freaks of nature. No surprise, the masters of propaganda repeatedly used the tidal wave metaphor in their communications in the months following the deadliest tsunami in history shook the world to its core with its colossal destruction in South East Asia. Talk about having no shame.

No matter how benevolent the image—or even the intention—may be, under it all their war strategy has relied on a tangled web of fear-inducing rhetoric that has confused the truth about family life. Not unlike the hoodwinking about reasons for war in Iraq, the latest spin was that homosexuals were the new weapons of mass destruction, capable of wiping out civilization with a single "I do." The message was: "marriage is under attack" by homosexual activists and needs protection via a constitutional amendment before it's too late. Little did they realize that their reverential creed of myths and misconceptions coded as traditional family values was more devastating to the health of marriage and family life than any gay lovebird will ever be.

As a marriage and family therapist, I'm down in the gritty trenches of domestic wars; and the view from here reveals a different truth. The simple fact is this: *The enemy lies within.* Marriages self-destruct. Sniping, silence, criticism and contempt are the deadly ammunition bringing marriages down, one at a time. This is a problem of the most personal sort, at the core of one's character and the heart of one's home. Any message to the contrary is not only deceptive, but turns people into helpless victims of irrelevant circumstance.

We have to ask, isn't it a bit ironic that the so-called "pro-family" camp, who tout the moral high ground, have forgotten that the responsibility for a sound family life lies squarely in the lap of the married? And, isn't it strange that those on this noble mission to defend marriage didn't bother to do a little bona fide research on the subject before trying to tinker with the U.S. Constitution?

Of course they didn't. There they would have found an abundance of evidence against their cause. Substantial findings from non-partisan research institutions and universities over the last twenty years suggest that good marriages—ones that are both satisfying and stable (i.e., "attack proof")—reflect the psychological makeup of the partners involved. Demographic research also shows that the highest percentage of divorce is *not* taking place among the notorious liberals from Massachusetts (the first state to legalize gay marriage and which has the *lowest* divorce rate in the nation), who are depicted by social conservatives as having their heads in ivory towers and morals in the gutter. According to a Pew Research Poll (2009)[23] the highest rate of divorce (and teen pregnancy, for that matter) lies in the Bible Belt states, at roughly 50% *above* the national average, where traditional family values thump away the loudest, setting the tone for the way things ought to be in the home and in the hood.

Why the contradiction? Because it's backwards; it's a beat that comes *not* from the inside out, but from the outside in. Rigid, authoritarian dogma imposes obedience and conformity, which ultimately comes at the expense of sound, full human development.

In chapters 5 and 6, I'll discuss morality in more detail. For now, suffice to say that an outside-in approach to moral development through controlling measures such as shame, punishment, black and white rules, and the fear of the wrath of God, doesn't facilitate proper brain *integration*. The basis of moral *integrity* and sound character begins here, where deep, personal meaning is created as values become woven into the soul. The traditional, patriarchal mode of imposing morality through obedience to authoritarian commands becomes, essentially, a superficial overlay that might look great on the surface, until that surface cracks.

This is why people as righteously right as Rush Limbaugh (with his three divorces and drug addiction), as haughtily holy as Pat Robertson with his hoard of hateful comments (WWJD, Pat?) and as scornful of secularists as Bill O'Reilly (who is no model of moral decorum, impulse control, civility *or* family values) just can't seem to follow their own blessed ideology. And let's not forget the constant storm of legal and ethical scandals raining down with some of our country's most prominent conservative religious leaders, politicians and close-knit cronies falling off their pious pedestals like drunks, with thuds that can be heard 'round the world.

There are many smack-on-the-forehead realizations to be found once we pull the string on this tightly spun rhetoric and see what we've got when it's all unwound. Take a Dramamine. You may get nauseous.

Gooey Terms and Loopy Logic

The repetitive refrain from the religious right has been that families are breaking down because of the failure to embrace traditional family values. Let's look at how this mantra has sucked many of us into the powerful vortex of rhetoric.

First, nobody wants families to break down, not gay people, not divorcees, not even the most jaded, liberal or unconventional among us. Now, add to the mix a little traditional family values toddy—a symbolic phrase warming the heart like a Norman Rockwell painting—and blissful, gauzy, images of family life inebriate the senses, sweeping us into a cozy fantasy of family fulfillment.

Clouding reality like this is highly effective for swaying favor, but useless at the end of the day when unpaid bills, piles of laundry, children pushing limits, and a spouse's annoying habits challenge us to our tongue-biting core. These lofty words are meaningless with no practical application, carrying no value other than the exquisite ability to manipulate voters.

One of my favorite examples of rhetorical nonsense was Tom Delay's response to the Federal Marriage Amendment failure to pass in the House of Representatives in 2004. As reported in the *New York Times* Delay warned, "If you destroy marriage as the definition of one man and one woman" children will not learn traditional values and "this country will go down."[24] What? I never heard of a definition destroying anything, let alone an entire society.

Loaded code words and phrases are designed to evoke emotions, while true meaning is glossed over. Everything sounds good, sounds right, sounds downright noble until you break the code and dig beneath the surface where the hidden agenda lies. The unspoken message behind the metaphorical wrapping is essentially a biblical one: we need to embrace fundamentalist religious beliefs or we will go straight to hell in a Puritan's hand basket.

In spite of their best efforts to instill fear and confound the senses, the religious right's cultural crusade will never come to fruition in a democratic society like ours. American principles are not seeded in religious fundamentalism and enforced by Taliban-like edicts, but founded on liberty and its counterpart, personal choice.

As democratic principles have slowly made their way into family life, patriarchal values have been edged out of the home like obsolete appliances. Marriage is no longer a duty, but a choice. The lock has been taken out of wedlock, making no-fault divorce legal. Women are no longer financially dependent upon "the man of the house." Domestic violence is no longer condoned or silenced. Even the distasteful label "bastard" no longer applies to children born to single mothers, but is reserved for those who rightfully earn it, like say, our favorite corporate criminals.

Without explicitly stating this (it would be the death of their mission), the religious right and their strategic political allies are at war, not with "amoral liberals" but with the cultural expression of democracy and the freedom it entails, threatening their authoritarian dominion. Strict patriarchal mores holding marriage and the nuclear family tightly in place have loosened considerably and religious fundamentalists don't like it one bit. This is a profound problem for them—but *not* The problem. The fact of the matter is that internally sound families remain standing, cultural buttresses propping them up or not. Healthy marriages stay together in spite of society's permission to divorce or gay people who want to marry.

The problems of family life have been ill-defined by the well meaning (perhaps) but not so well informed, simplistically reduced into a neat little rhetorical package dubbed "the family values crisis." And, with the finest circular reasoning available, these self-ordained authorities preach a "return to traditional family values" as the answer. How's that for getting to the bottom of things? No wonder problems have persisted, and families have been in "crisis" for the better part of forty years.

Turning the Problem Inside Out

If we really want to understand why nuclear families have been imploding at an astounding rate for the last four decades, it's time to take a fresh look at the problem. Perhaps nuclear families are breaking down not because of "liberal" values, but for some other yet unidentified reason. Maybe conventional assumptions about what it means to be a good family or raise well-adjusted children have been off-kilter. Maybe so-called traditional family values rather than being the solution are actually part of the problem, holding unseen flaws compromising the core of family life, landing us exactly where we are today.

Shouldn't we be asking: If the nuclear family is so ideal, why in the world is it falling apart? What works, works, doesn't it? Could it be possible that the nuclear family isn't so ideal? After all, the nuclear family is not even traditional, merely a passing trend in the history of American culture. As family historian Stephanie Coontz, explains in her illuminating book, *The Way We Never Were*,[25] the nuclear family structure, although idealized and mythologized as traditional, was a mere blip in America mid 20th Century, enjoying a brief period of statistical normality then collapsing like a house of cards when the winds of social change began to blow.

Coontz describes how the nuclear family emerged with the prosperity that followed WWII when people began driving off into the suburbs in spiffy new automobiles, leaving extended families behind. These became the *new* family values and nuclear families became the faddish ideal, right along side Swanson's TV dinners—nicely packaged, with neat little compartments keeping everything in its place...no fuss, no muss, and easy disposal of that which is no longer of use—including extended family.

We have to ask: did we let our zealous consumerism that mushroomed in the '50s create a cultural shift in family values that was ultimately a mistake? For 99% of our time on this planet we've lived in hunter-gather societies where the ratio of adults to children was 4:1. As renowned cultural anthropologist Margaret Mead has noted, "Nobody has ever before asked the nuclear family to live all by itself in a box the way we do. With no relatives, no support, we've put it in an impossible situation." Could it be, perhaps, that living in isolated units without extended family and close, intimate communities not only isn't traditional, but a set up for struggle if not failure?

I think so. Research suggests that extended networks of close relationships are integral to overall life satisfaction. On a more personal note, I know my husband and I would have had less stress, more time for sweet nothings and making love with a couple of extra sets of hands on deck. This can do wonders for a marriage, and by extension, a family. Compound the losing ratio built into the nuclear family structure with the modern-day financial necessity for dual-career families and suddenly the extraordinary burden becomes clear. The load is ridiculous and making time for meaningful, soul-nourishing, slow-down-and-connect quality of personal relationships nearly impossible.

Nuclear families are breaking down not because of a failure to embrace traditional family values but because of the inability to successfully navigate the emotional terrain of everyday lives and find meaningful, soulful sustenance in the process. This is a Herculean challenge under the best of circumstances, yet has been made even more so by our increasingly sped-up, media-saturated, consumer-oriented, bottom-line driven, financially stressed, sleep-deprived, time-stretched, technology-addicted, socially isolated, spiritually devoid culture.

Most folks *are* going to the altar, getting married, and trying to create the nuclear family ideal. Yet, the odds for a lasting marriage are no better than a crapshoot, with approximately half ending in divorce. The glitch: We've been lured into a fantasy, told to create an image that simply asserts how the family structure should appear (first comes love, then comes marriage, then comes a baby in a baby carriage) with no real understanding of what it actually takes to create happy homes, healthy souls and well-adjusted children.

Traditional family values that put an emphasis on institutional conformity—form over function, roles over the quality of relationships, and obedience to dogma over inner personal and spiritual development—are actually *shallow values* contributing to a hole in the soul of families today. As Thomas Moore notes, the essence a family life lies much deeper than form, and yearns to be fed on the level of soul.

"A family is not an abstract cultural ideal: a man, woman and children living blissfully in a mortgaged house on a quiet neighborhood street. The family the soul wants is a felt network of relationship, an evocation of a certain kind of interconnection that grounds, roots and nestles.

"It is possible to live in a family structure that doesn't evoke the image of the family that the soul craves; soul doesn't automatically follow structure. We may also discover that a particular family doesn't need to reproduce the ideal family in order to give the soul what it needs."[26]

The solution lies *not* in reinforcing external edicts holding families in place with laws as the religious right is determined to do with their judicial jujitsu. Rather, the solution lies in strengthening families from the inside out, building inner integrity based on solid character that can withstand and resolve the sometimes stormy, often raw, and always complex emotional elements of family life.

This problem is much too old, consequences too grave, and current research too compelling to continue clinging to false beliefs. It's time to re-evaluate what's really going on in family life—to dispel the myths and examine the misconceptions, and to introduce new ways of understanding and solving the four-decades long crisis in family life with its negative effects rippling across our culture.

3
Mother of all Myths
The 1950's Nuclear Family Ideal

"The great enemy of the truth is very often not the lie—
deliberate, contrived, and dishonest, but the myth—
persistent, persuasive, and realistic."

John F. Kennedy

The image of the traditional nuclear family prominent in the 1950's has been painted in our collective psyches as a nostalgic ideal, an aspiration many hold as they set out to create a family: father, mother and children cocooning together in suburbia, away from the grit and grime of society's dark underbelly. It's a comfortable living where clean streets, pristine yards and single-family homes provide the setting to raise wholesome children and carry out daily lives in bliss, with nary a need unmet. If you have a traditional nuclear family all will be *swell*, just as it was for Beaver Cleaver.

Social conservatives promote this nostalgia to swoon voters. But what we really have here is a vague, faulty notion of healthy family life based on hallowed myths, misconceptions and fantasies of what family is, should be, and must be. While we're lovingly attached to this mythic nuclear family ideal, believing in its curative power to wrest our country from moral decline, it doesn't seem to be working, nor ever did.

As Stephanie Coontz recounts in *The Way We Never Were*, what *is* true about this period is that Americans were prospering, and all seemed swell in America's peachy keen world. After centuries of struggle for survival, the darkness of the Great Depression, and the taxing effects of two world wars, middle-class Americans were financially prospering and could finally relish "the good life."[27]

Ironically, it was during this era symbolizing traditional family values that people actually nixed old-world values. As Coontz explains, with disposable income in hand, people fled cozy, extended family togetherness in urban centers and on rural farms, chasing the American dream of homeownership.[28] Family farms were uprooted for neatly paved neighborhoods while grandparents, aunts, uncles, and cousins were jettisoned, no longer needed. Pretty picket fences popped into place in newly sprouting suburbs, proudly defining personal property and cordoning families into discrete entities. Mother, father and children, like the nucleus of an atom, were then considered to be the essential elements of family life. The concept of the nuclear family was born.

The outside world penetrated homes through a powerful new medium, television. As if partaking in a mystical experience, families huddled in their respective living rooms, transfixed by the images emanating from a box with antenna ears. Advertisers scooped rapt Americans into the palms of their hands, molding their values and very desires. From pink toilet paper to Betty Crocker cake mix, from spiffy home appliances to shiny new automobiles, Americans could have it all. Consumerism and material possessions took on paramount importance,[29] and "keeping up with the Joneses'" became a national pastime.

As families became isolated from extended relatives and from intimate, personal engagement in their day-to-day lives, Americans tuned into shows like *Donna Reed, Ozzie and Harriet* and *Father Knows Best* for involvement in the family life of others. Offering glimpses into the private worlds of fictional families, these shows became our country's reference points, and a new standard, a new way to "keep up with the Joneses," was born.

Family life on television was propagandized, portrayed as sterile, dispassionate, unruffled and unreal. Marriages were characterized as asexual domestic arrangements with twin beds in the conjugal bedroom, always neatly made, appearing never slept in, let alone having sex in. Housewives were clad in aprons with dresses and pearls while presiding over sparkling kitchens. Children were clean-scrubbed and eagerly obedient. Harmonious and happy home life was the image projected, where conflicts were comedic and easily resolved. It was an era depicted as nice 'n tidy. Everything and everyone fit in a box.

But life's not that neat. Never is. Never was.

With families tucked away behind pretty picket fences, family boundaries became more distinct and family secrets more tightly held, operating to protect a coveted image. The realities of family life rarely, if ever, surfaced. A caricature of family life became the ideal. The ideal became a myth. The myth became the truth. And no one wanted to admit otherwise. "What would the neighbors think?" became a cultural mantra; societal shame was used to enforce conformity and obedience in an attempt to keep families and children in check.

Did it work?

In my research, I came across a startling statistic. A government report published in 1960 read:

"[Juvenile delinquency] is increasing in suburban areas, and the rate of increase there is higher than that in the central city. The present rate of increase in the number of cases coming before juvenile courts is about five times among young people aged ten to seventeen. If the present trend continues unabated, it has been estimated that by 1970, one boy in every five will be involved in at least one court delinquency during his adolescence."[30]

This from an era that television had mythologized with *Happy Days* wholesomeness? Could that era have been a bit romanticized? The fuzzier the memory, the brighter the picture, perhaps?

Astute cultural observers have seen beyond the pristine whitewash. One *Time* magazine essayist writing about Bob Hope's success observed that the '50s were "the great age of denial" perfectly suited for the type of humor Bob Hope embodied. He was described as:

"...the voice of 20th Century America at mid-passage, the spokesman of our heedless, surface skimming-spirit, the comic for the age of the production line, churning out interchangeable, immediately disposable jokes at an industrial pace."[31]

The author emphasized that Bob Hope had breadth, but not depth. He was the perfect entertainer for a time when instant gratification rather than meaningful truths drove the culture. It was, in short, an era with no soul.

Rapid economic growth created a focus on the all mighty dollar, while rigid conformity created role-based inauthenticity. Combined, these shallow values hollowed out the soul of society. As Gerald Celente, author of *Trends* notes, prejudice, repression of feeling, and allegiance to the status quo were the subterranean currents of mid-century reality. Reflecting on the 1950's, Celente states:

"...beyond the economic prosperity, for those who remembered accurately, it was not wall-to-wall Ozzie and Harriet *at all. It was a time of racism, McCarthyism, and J. Edgar Hooversism. Women's rights, civil rights and gay rights existed mostly in the minds of visionaries. It was a time of hypocrisy, sexual, political, and social repression, and blind conformity."*[32]

Just as we have rightfully questioned the virtue of Wonder Bread, that beloved staple of 1950's cuisine, perhaps we should wonder about family life back then as well. All must not have been so wonderful if the Cultural Revolution surfaced a mere decade or so later.

As Celente goes on to say...

"If fifties family values had been real, there would have been no sixties revolution. It would have been impossible for a few unarmed and powerless malcontents (weren't they dubbed the Peaceniks, after all?) to disrupt a basically harmonious society. Prosperity masked the malaise for two decades but could not cure it."[33]

The classic film, *The Graduate*, captured the cultural malaise of the 1950's, zeroing in on the zeitgeist of the times with just one word delivered to an earnest young man searching for direction in his life.

Mr. McGuire:	I just want to say one word to you— just one word.
Ben:	Yes sir.
Mr. McGuire:	Are you listening?
Ben:	Yes I am.
Mr. McGuire:	Plastics.[34]

A false, plastic quality pervaded a culture becoming more and more enamored with mass production that was fast, cheap, and artificial, lacking heart and soul, quality and substance. It was a culture becoming obsessed with bottom line success, corporate profits and capitalistic strivings—the very values that Ben was questioning. He represented a generation aching to escape a meaningless world that focused on "having," consuming, achieving, one-upping.

These shallow cultural values that began trickling into family life during the 1950's have reached flood-level proportions today. As seen in this film's depiction of Ben's upper-middle class family, there was money but no intimacy. They didn't know their son— they didn't know what his dreams were, or what made him light up. They had no idea of the fears and doubts he harbored, having been newly inaugurated into manhood with his diploma finally in hand. His parents' greatest pride was in showcasing Ben and his spectacular Ivy League accomplishments to their friends. Ben's lack of soulful, meaningful connection to his family, to others, to life was clear. It was the essence of his anguished struggle, and it spoke to an entire generation searching for something more.

This "something," I believe, is *soul*. As Thomas Moore describes it: "Soul is not a thing, but a quality or a dimension of experiencing life and ourselves. It has to do with depth, value, and relatedness, heart and personal substance."[35] Could the soul have been neglected in routine nuclear family home life of the '50s, like it was in Ben's family? What were the predominant trends and characteristics of families in this hallowed, yet hollow, time?

Husbands, having grown up themselves in a tradition that didn't allow men to express feelings, were pragmatic and often emotionally unavailable, having been expected to check their softer side early in boyhood. They served as patriarchal commanders-in-chief of the home. "Wait 'til your father gets home" was a familiar refrain. Being the breadwinner by bringing home a paycheck constituted being a good husband and father, not communication or affectionate bonding. Connection was distant, stiff and role-based, making relationships superficial and perfunctory.

Since premarital sex was stigmatized, it was the leading reason young people married.[36] It's hard not to wonder about the sincerity of any marriage that might be based on a desire to "get some." Then, in the quest for carnal knowledge, people tiptoed around sex because of puritanical cultural taboos, making the experience fraught with ignorance, discontent and distance between partners. While sexuality is one of the most natural of human expressions and desires, it was perceived as something shameful, remote and perhaps even mechanical, reflecting the personality of mid-century culture. (Today, we have soulless, objectifying sexuality run amok yet without the cultural shame.)

When the war years ended, men flooded into the United States job market and women were encouraged back into the home.[37] Rosie the Riveter morphed into Harriet the Homemaker, the new bourgeois female ideal. Men pursued the goal of higher education via the GI Bill[38], and women sought a man to provide them with house and home. After the war, the age of marriage and motherhood fell drastically.[39] It's very possible that without an opportunity to fully develop an independent adult identity before getting married, the ability of women to have strong, healthy, equal partnerships with their mates was diminished.

Unlike earlier eras, mothering became the purpose, and children the sole focus, of women's lives. Without other channels for closeness or help with daily routines from extended families, dissatisfaction, isolation and stress took hold. Mothers found "little helpers" courtesy of the pharmaceutical industry, the cutesy name given to an ugly drug that packed a powerful punch. The culture of denial helped usher in a hidden phenomenon of Valium-abusing housewives who acquired the requisite patience for their perpetually selfless duties at a price. Tranquilizer abuse was almost non-existent in 1955, then reached almost 1.5 million pounds sold in 1959.[40]

Of course, not all mothers coped by popping pills. Nevertheless, the magnitude of female distress was tremendous. The torrent of response to Betty Friedan's, *The Feminine Mystique*,[41] gave voice to the ennui and dissonance many women were feeling in the supposedly ideal life that mid-20th Century culture had created for them. Women began to wake up with a roar, heralding a powerful uprising that became the women's liberation movement.

Once the happy housewife myth was cracked open, unpleasant facts about nuclear family life began tumbling out of the closet over the next couple of decades. And this was some pretty dirty laundry. Alcoholism, domestic violence, child abuse, and various other forms of family dysfunction were suddenly on our radar screen. The true family and marital experiences of many were revealed, recalibrating what constituted normal family life, prompting a stunning zero-to-sixty divorce rate fitting of a NASCAR track. No sir-ee. All was *not* peachy keen in this fabled world.

With the clear-eyed perceptiveness depicted in the timeless tale, *The Emperor's New Clothes*, children of the '50s and '60s had witnessed a different reality behind those shuttered windows, knowing *something* wasn't right. *Something* was missing. But it wasn't as obvious as a silly little emperor romping around in all his royal nakedness. It was a truth difficult to articulate, a subtle sense that a holy façade was veiling a not-so-glorious reality.

In a natural quest to separate from their elders, this generation's youth began to assert themselves, breaking cultural taboos in an effort to seek deeper truths and greater meaning. Pulling away from a tradition that demanded emotions be repressed and individuality suppressed, they bucked their way into adulthood. With the youthful spirit of rebellion bumping into a culture of institutional conformity and authoritarian moralism, the stage was set for the '60's backlash.

When ongoing government corruption at the expense of young Americans' lives was exposed in the course of the Vietnam War, the burgeoning impulse to challenge authority was unleashed, and the counterculture movement was born. Anti-war protests exploded across the country, bras were flung far and wide in the name of women's liberation, and LSD was dropped in a mystical search to "find oneself." Conformity was rejected and personal problems were laid bare, dragged out of the home and onto the streets for all to see.

As social conservatives would tell it, this was the beginning of the end of decency. As I see it, the pendulum had swung too far left, as far to the loose left as it was to the tight right. But the youth of this era were on to something. With the natural developmental quest to cross boundaries and explore the unknown, the baby boomers had a wide-eyed desire to search for a greater truth. Unfortunately, as one would expect from the not-yet-mature, they lacked a refined approach neither seasoned by experience nor filtered by sound judgment. Caught up in the passion of their mission, they became not so innocent and looked not so wise.

There are many subtle, yet profound, problems with traditional family values embedded in and symbolized by 1950's conformity—patriarchal, authoritarian values that continue to be pitched with fervor by social conservatives today out of a perverse nostalgia for something that never really existed. Although often tossed aside by many as irrelevant to life in the new millennium, these insidious myths and misconceptions continue to impact us as they have been intricately woven into cultural lore with threads of such beliefs residing in each and every one of us, in families that look traditional, as well as in those that don't.

My hope is that the valuable elements of an important cause, lost in the raucous debauchery of the reactionary 60's, can finally be realized. But it will take thoughtful responses today as opposed to the knee-jerk reactions of yore, kicking every crotchety conservative ideal in sight. And, it will take clear eyes. If we look back on the 50's without nostalgic yearnings blurring the edges, we can see that what we've deemed traditional isn't and wasn't. What we've deemed ideal, isn't and wasn't.

There's nothing ideal about a soulless culture. It's how and why we've landed where we are today—sinking deeper and deeper into the same spiritual sinkhole of the 1950's. As Einstein famously said, "Problems cannot be solved at the same level of awareness that created them." It's time to ditch the myth and see this era anew.

In some ways our attachment to these distorted views is peculiar and in other ways not, given our human tendency to turn the past into glory days. There's a coziness in softening cold, harsh facts with warm and fuzzy nostalgia. But having values based on nothing more than this grounds us like an untethered rope. What we're left with are families floating apart in a society morally adrift. If we hope to strengthen cultural mores and family life, we have to anchor ourselves in a solid, clear understanding and *principled* definition of this elusive yet critical concept, family values.

4
Redefining Family Values
From Dubious Values to Valuable Principles

"When we value correct principles, we have truth—
a knowledge of things as they are."

Stephen Covey

U p until now, the term "family values" has been co-opted by the religious right—coined by them, used by them, promoted by them, owned by them. The meaning and validity of their so-called family values have never been analyzed, just assumed to be good because they are values related to family. Yet, before we can understand what constitutes good or wholesome family values, we have to get clear on what it is we're actually talking about.

When the phrase "family values" is employed as heart-tugging rhetoric, the very critical word "values" is used in a not-so-helpful way. As Webster's Dictionary defines it:

"the ideals, customs, institutions, etc., of a society toward which the people of the group have an affective regard. These values may be positive as cleanliness, freedom, education, etc., or negative as cruelty, crime or blasphemy."[42]

With this use of the word, there are serious shortcomings. These types of values can be positive or negative, based on subjective, loosely defined affectations. This means we have arbitrary standards defining ideals—not a sturdy or useful tool to dig our culture out of a mess. Secondly, "affective regard" for an ideal means nothing in terms of actual value that has any merit beyond preference. I love chocolate. My ideal meal is chocolate morning, noon and night, with a pizza thrown in every now and then for dessert—not much nutritional merit, regardless of how much I value it.

What if, for the sake of argument, these ideals were born out of dogmatic attachment to tradition, or a skewed sense of normal— say I lived in a culture (ahem) where subsisting on pizza, chocolate and chemically laced fast food was considered the standard way of life, the way you were supposed to eat. Would that suddenly give these foods greater true value? Not a chance.

In order to usefully define family values, we have to turn to a different type of value determined by principles rather than personal preferences, ideology or cultural opinions. This alternative type of value defined by Webster's is: "to consider with respect to worth, excellence, usefulness, or importance."[43] *Now* we're getting somewhere.

The way we have used family values rhetoric as an apple-pie-in-the-American-sky ideal, does nothing for solving real problems or offering worth beyond a feel-good sugar high, an empty dream of happiness ever after that has no substance. But when an ideal is chosen because of its usefulness or function, as opposed to dearly held myths and entrenched beliefs, it takes on an entirely different kind of value. Now we have a true value based on *objective principles* that serve a purpose greater than defense of preferences, ideology or status quo.

Stephen Covey, in his book *The Seven Habits of Highly Effective People*, deftly clarifies the distinction between principles and values: "Principles are not values. A gang of thieves can share values, but they are in violation of the fundamental principles ..." He likens principles to territory and values to maps, explaining that values, like maps, are idiosyncratic ways of seeing or interpreting the territory, which may or may not be accurate. Being subjective in nature, maps can be incorrect, but the territory is never incorrect. The key is to know the territory, the universal, fundamental principles, for when we do, "we have truth—a knowledge of things as they are."[44]

What I'm suggesting is that we come to know the nitty-gritty territory of family life, not the fluff and puff of which rhetoric is made, or the grand illusions on which ideology hang. When we do, we'll understand the core principles necessary for creating emotionally healthy families and children, and by extension, a sound society.

One of Covey's cardinal rules for effective living is to "begin with the end in mind." With ultimate purpose of family life in mind, we can then determine a true and correct course, a way of seeing the territory clearly, a view free of ideology that blinds, distorts, and confuses what is simply so. Otherwise, we end up following a vague and faulty map leading us where we never intended to go, thinking we're on the way to "happiness ever after" and then suddenly find ourselves in divorce courts, rehab centers, and therapist offices with bewildered and messed-up children in tow.

In order to understand the family values problem, we need to turn this meaningless phrase on its head and ask: What is the purpose of family life? What is its function? And, what does it really take to achieve this goal? When we answer these questions, we can begin to speak of real family values, those values of value that are based on solid principles of human development and family relations. From here we can define a gold standard that actually makes sense, and come to understand why traditional family values—those patriarchal values seeded over two thousand years ago—may be antithetical to the purpose of family life today.

"It's the Function, Stupid"

It's time to make the right wing's family values monologue into an intelligent dialogue. Only then can we inject into the argument what professionals in the field have known for thirty-plus years: *the family is not a static, role-based institution, but a dynamic, emotionally driven system whose function is critical for survival.* And like all open living systems, families must evolve if they are to survive.

As culture and society have transformed over the millennia, the function of marriage and family life has transformed as well, from a social system geared toward ensuring tribal survival, to meeting higher order human needs. In Western democracies today, the purpose of family life is to provide for the optimal development of its members. With this end in mind, "family values of value" are those principles that lead us toward the realization of this ultimate goal: *optimal development*. How well a family functions to achieve this purpose determines the value, health, or "goodness" of families, regardless of form—Left, Right, gay, straight, religious or secular.

Without getting into the abstract elements of systems theory which reveal complex processes regulating emotional closeness and distance between family members (i.e., feedback loops and dialectical tensions of change and homeostasis, etc.), the question of importance is this: What exactly *is* a well-functioning family?

The Beavers Scale of Family Health (sadly, no relation to *Leave It to Beaver*) developed by psychiatrist W. Robert Beavers and colleagues at Southern Methodist University has been widely used as a family diagnostic and assessment tool validated with decades of research. It's been one of the most reliable instruments to objectively measure and classify the functional quality of family life. Five levels of family health have been delineated along a spectrum, from Level I, which approximates optimal functioning to Level V, deemed the most disturbed level.[45]

The Level I, optimally functioning family, is an open system, which means it's continually adapting to its context (culture and society) and the changing dynamics and needs of its parts (family members and their development). Like all functioning systems, it strikes a balance between chaos and rigidity, change and homeostasis.

What does all this actually mean in terms of family life? The family has rules, but the rules are flexible. If there are two parents/

partners, power is shared. Communication is open, direct and clear. Boundaries are respected and conflicts are easily resolved. The adults in the family honor and consider the opinions, feelings and values of the children. Essentially, healthy families are democratically organized and inspired, with humanistic values being the governing force.

There is no "children should be seen and not heard" mentality here, there's no allegiance to "proper" gender roles or institutional form, and there's no charge of obedience to "the man of the house," dogma, nor God the Father. It doesn't take a specialist in family studies to conclude that these optimal criteria in no way approximate traditional, patriarchal values let alone religious fundamentalists' interpretation of them.

At the other end of the spectrum is Level V, classified as the least healthy family system characterized by chaos and disorganization with no overt rules, or rules that are inconsistent and arbitrary. Communication is rarely clear, direct or properly received and responded to. Typically there are multiple types of problems in these families, such as substance abuse and/or severe mental and personality disorders that render emotional stability, trust and secure attachment, the bases of psychological health, nearly impossible.

It's important to recognize that any form of family—traditional or not, religious or not—can have characteristics of either extreme, Level I or Level V. It's not the form that matters. What's indicative of healthy family functioning are the emotional dynamics that determine whether or not the basic human needs for secure attachment, meaningful connection, and communal belonging are met, while allowing for the development of healthy autonomy.

The Level III family, which is known as the "rule-bound family," most closely approximates traditional, patriarchal family values in all their glory. While this is conceptually in the middle of the Beavers scale, the effects of such a family system should not be misconstrued as normal or even good enough. In fact, this type of family is significantly problematic, in many ways directly contradicting a well-functioning family. It's better viewed as the flipside of the chaotic family system. (Visually expressed, imagine a spectrum that splits like a tuning fork on one end, with healthy family functioning on the singular end, and two possible pathways on the dysfunctional side of the spectrum, the upper path being the rule-bound family and the lower path being the even more dysfunctional chaotic family system.)

Rather than having arbitrary, inconsistent, or a flat-out absence of rules, the "rule-bound" family system is authoritarian and rigid, a "strict father" orientation operating with the predominant goal of controlling individuality. In these types of families there is an emphasis on reinforcing hierarchal structures, roles, obedience and "family loyalty" (i.e., believe what we believe, do what we want you to do, don't deviate from convention, don't challenge our authority, our values, etc.).

Here, conformity is the name of the game, and authoritarianism is the overriding rule, often coming at the expense of a truly close, loving relationship. As the late Conway Twitty expressed in his song, "That's My Job:"

"Later we barely got along
This teenage boy and he
Most of the fights it seems
Were over different dreams
We each held for me."[46]

While the rule-bound family might proclaim love for each other and appear to operate effectively, it's a system that is fundamentally askew, propelled by conditional love that doesn't provide for the optimal development of its members, short-circuiting something known as individuation or differentiation—psychologically sound, autonomous development that, among other things, makes a person capable of healthy, mature love. Author and libertarian intellectual Ayn Rand put it most simply in her novel *Fountainhead*: "To say 'I love you,' one must know first how to say the 'I.'"[47] In developmental terms, we would say one must have a strong sense of self, or healthy ego integration (not to be confused with egotistic self-centeredness).

Although often not recognized, the havoc raised by rule-bound families is profound. Individuals growing up in these types of families learn that the way to resolve conflicts is not through honesty and emotional vulnerability, but through manipulation and intimidation, or conversely, deference and avoidance. Dysfunction does exist on a continuum, and it would be fair to say that the more dysfunctional, the more potential harm is created. However, no matter the level of dysfunction, when relationships are perceived as unsafe, individuals learn to turn away from others, rather than toward them for emotional comfort, picking up self-soothing habits as substitutes (i.e., addictions and compulsions) and bristly or withdrawing interpersonal patterns that keep others away, serving to protect a fragile sense of self—all of which interfere with intimacy.

Tragically, the consequences don't stop there. When defenses such as these are born, a domino effect is experienced through the generations. Dysfunctional families beget emotionally and psychologically scarred offspring who beget dysfunctional families. Unless of course, the cycle is corrected through remedial measures involving personal growth and change.

Emotional dynamics, the fuel that drives all family systems, are the external expression of internal psychodynamics—a fancy term that suggests we carry around a psychic blueprint developed in early relationships that then becomes the reference point for later relationships, affecting the ways we react and interact in relationships. While this line of reasoning has been around since the time of Freud, current brain neuroscience research is supporting such theories, showing how the quality of early attachment relationships affects brain development and determines how we process cognitions, emotions and interpersonal perceptions which profoundly influence later relationships—particularly those in which we are the most emotionally vulnerable or have the most at stake.

While not all divorces are a result of maladaptive psychodynamic processes (or "bugs in the programming" as I like to say), they are a major contributor to chronic marital distress and the divorce pandemic. Numerous well-documented and rigorous studies have shown that relationship skills, or lack thereof, determines the likelihood of divorce. Through longitudinal research at the University of Washington, John Gottman has been able to predict, with 94% accuracy, which couples will eventually divorce. His criteria point to the *emotional quality* of the relationship, distilling it down to two basic areas: 1) how conflict is handled, and 2) how much fondness is expressed during non-conflict times.[48]

The soundness of family life is determined by emotional dynamics, and more specifically, the quality of intimacy available in the family system, where all feelings are accepted and each family member's unique humanity can unfold. In these families, individual differences are not seen as threatening and being oneself is not seen as badness or a betrayal of the family (unlike authoritarian families where conformity is the goal). When the basic human need for personal autonomy is met while an intimate, safe and secure connection with family members is preserved, children and families can thrive.[49]

In terms of family function, something becomes abundantly clear: family values of real value are not about protecting institutions, enforcing religious dogma, valuing definitions, or prohibiting gay people from getting married. Fundamentally, family life is not about traditional structural conformity, institutional togetherness, or biblical mandate. It's not even about the right to be or look different.

The family is ultimately about affairs of the heart. In no other social realm are emotions more tender, complicated, and influential in determining the psychological and neurobiological fate of children. Yet, we've ignored the profound nuances of this critical interconnection, the *emotional quality* of family life, as if families were nothing more than a one-dimensional, role-based social unit. We've erroneously come to equate proper (i.e., traditional) family structure as goodness, even when the relationships are damaging or depleting, thoughtless or callous, self-involved or over-involved—coming from a lack of inner wisdom, a lack of soulful awareness of self and others, devoid of the type of real loved needed for optimum health and growth.

It's time to wake up to the profound influence the emotional quality of family relations has on human development and the development of the soul, and shed the conventional, patriarchal notions that attempt to control from the outside in, which precludes loving, respectful acknowledgment of one's unique humanity. The focus needs to shift to that which honors the human need for sound attachment, where deep, meaningful connection lies, nurturing the soul. When we get this, true family values are within our reach.

The Pearls and Perils of Tradition

Tradition, with its routine and order, provides us with predictable comfort, soothing like a rocking chair. Back and forth. Back and forth. No need to worry about what is to come next, because this always follows that. It's simply the way it's done, and always has been done. No need to think, because the thinking has been done for us. No need to search for truths, because truth has been laid out before us.

While tradition provides a well-worn groove, allowing us to glide along without undue effort or concern about veering into uncharted territories, it can also provide a false sense of security because change and adaptation are facts of life. While tradition can provide purpose, it can also turn followers into sheep, disconnected from their own sense of meaning, tranquilized by ritual, numb to what really matters. And in terms of family life, honoring tradition can come at the expense of honoring each other, interfering with truly close, loving, personal relationships.

One of the most artful illustrations of tension between adherence to tradition, the need for adaptation, and the impact on family relationships is the 1964 award-winning Broadway musical, *Fiddler on the Roof.* [50] It's a story about how, in a changing culture, the beloved bonds of tradition that hold a family together may also threaten to break a family apart.

The story is set in a remote Russian village at the turn of the 20th Century. With modern ideas and attitudes beginning to infiltrate the villagers' sheltered world, their traditions are challenged and their lives are thrown off balance. Tevye, a family patriarch, has three daughters on the cusp of adulthood. As they are exposed to these worldly influences, they begin adopting their own ideas about life and begin to shun some of their culture's traditions. When his daughters' choose suitors who defy their father's idea of a proper match, Tevye turns away from his daughters, rejecting them in anger and fear. He is torn between devotion to the traditional values that have sustained him his entire life, and his love for his daughters. This crisis sets the stage for his evolution as a spiritual man, which ironically, required him to shed his dogmatic religious traditions.

Tevye eventually rises above the challenges his cultural context and family placed on him. While tradition functioned to give his life meaning, he comes to realize that ultimately meaning has to come from within, and a stubborn grip on tradition can derail someone from a deeper purpose—love and acceptance.

By succumbing to the trance of tradition, the soul of family life can disappear without missing a beat in the everyday routine of supposedly loving family life. This point is dramatized in the play when Tevye asks his oft-disagreeable wife, Golde, "Do you love me?" And she replies, "Do I whaaat???," then launches into song about her years of faithful adherence to her domestic duties (cleaning, cooking, etc.), which had become a substitute for a personal expression of love that is full of *feeling*—vulnerable, raw, real—not duty and role bound.

There is great comfort that comes from traditions that compel rote function, like the fiddler who climbed up on that roof everyday with fiddle in hand because that is just what you do, logic be damned. But by steadfastly clutching to tradition, we can create an imbalanced state as life moves forward prompting change and adaptation. The danger is that tradition can overshadow inner wisdom and awareness of that which is most meaningful. This was tenderly touched upon when Tevye sings the song, *Sunrise, Sunset* on the eve of his daughter's wedding, reminiscing on her childhood.

Tevya was forced to examine his beliefs through the truths in his heart. At first he was livid about his daughters' willful independence, denying them his love. As his character transforms, he eventually sheds his coveted ideals and lets go of his dogmatic notions of what his daughters *ought* to be doing, feeling, thinking by letting go of his anger and fear. He had to choose between patriarchal control of them and genuine love for them by honoring their human right to freedom and happiness.

This is what healthy family functioning is about: being grounded at the soul and operating from a place of inner wisdom.

The wholesomeness of family life does not depend on form or definition or what your sexual orientation is. Rather, healthy family life comes from within, involving a quality of character that allows us to relate from a place of love rather than fear. To rise above fear-based reactions and mindfully respond is a ultimately a transcendent experience, a non-dogmatic value that cuts across any and all religions.

This is faith, pure and simple. This type of trust in the face of fear is what allows us to love, to be truly intimate, tender, and compassionate in our family lives. Without the virtues of wisdom and faith of this sort, we're apt to be reactive and shallow, mindlessly operating in relation to each other, fleeing to the comforting constraints of rote traditions, mindlessly rocking back and forth, back and forth, lulled into a comforting, albeit deadening, trance.

It's this particular quality of character and love that we need to bring into our discussion about family values, a quality of relationship that has been overlooked by conventional wisdom, political rhetoric and religious doctrine. It's what M. Scott Peck refers to in his classic book, *The Road Less Traveled*, as a type of love that requires *personal discipline*.[51] It's a soulful grounding and connection in oneself that allows for a rich quality of relationship to others, a mindful relating that enhances intimacy between partners and that anchors the developing psyche of one's offspring. It's an interpersonal experience of empathy and attunement. It's the type of love needed if we hope for children and marriages to thrive. It's the road we better get on soon, if we hope to find solutions that feed the soul of family life and produce sound children and upstanding citizens.

Fiddler on the Roof illuminates the complexity of cultural traditions and family values that look "right," yet ultimately limit optimum personal development. Some of the more obvious examples such as matchmaking and strict adherence to gender roles (i.e., ruler/keeper of the house) we have long ago changed. But other more subtle forces, like the way we love or reject one another due to fear and our own unidentified ego needs, continues strong today, lurking just beneath the surface.

If we want to create healthy, functional families, we have to begin defining family values as those values that give attention to our inner emotional and spiritual worlds. While Tevye had to question the dogmatic injunctions of his religion and eventually defy them, he transcended spiritually by embracing these values:

> *"The fruit of the Spirit is love, joy, peace, patience, kindness, goodness, faithfulness, gentleness, and self-control."* [52]

While these *values of value* do come from the Bible, they are not the same authoritarian values that family values advocates proclaim, now are they? Let's untangle the utter mess that is the Bible as it relates to so-called family values.

Biblical Family Values: Does Righteous Make Right?

Family values advocates have prescribed a "return to traditional family values" as the antidote to family troubles today. It's an appealing notion at first glance, but if we read the label on this sweet-smelling tonic, we'll find that the fine print exacts a return to unsavory biblical beliefs. This is never explicitly stated because this is not an easy sell—it was a barbaric time, in an ancient culture, in stark contrast to modern-day realities and sensibilities.

While euphemized as traditional family values, the biblical beliefs to which they are referring are steeped in an outdated patriarchal culture that viewed wives as possessions, often one of many, whose sole purpose was to serve their husband, along with his many concubines. A woman's first and foremost job was to bear children to ensure progeniture, a means of carrying forth the man's name and creating a bloodline through which to pass property. In this pre-scientific period in history, it was believed that semen carried the full potential of new life, where the sperm only needed a womb in which to be planted so that the man's seed may grow. It was a time when lifespans were short, and propagation equated survival by strengthening the tribe with sheer numbers against others competing for dominance and power.

It was a time when the rape of a woman was a crime not against her, but against her father and/or husband. A time when girls as young as the age of their first menstruation became fair game, handed over to a man chosen for her by others, perhaps even at birth. Marriage was not about love. It was about duty to husbands, to fathers, to tribal patriarchy.[53]

While the Bible is billed as the ultimate rule book for family virtue, the most savage expression of patriarchal family values are promoted by it: the stoning to death of non-virginal brides, adulteresses, and rebellious children for their failure to obey husbands, fathers, and commandments from on high. Were these functional values, values of worth, usefulness, excellence or importance? I suppose you could say they were functional—in an archaic society invested in wielding control, crucial to ensuring the hierarchical dominance of men, kings, and God the Father. But, tyrannical command and killing women and children aren't exactly ways to optimize their development.

Was it a moral system? Hardly. As these examples show, such beliefs are profoundly devoid of common human decency and humanistic concerns, which must lie at the heart of any truly moral system. Although commonly used interchangeably, values and morals are not one and the same, and should never be construed as such.

While Christian fundamentalists use the Bible to support their brand of family values, oddly enough, the New Testament makes absolutely *no* reference to family values; and the Old Testament tells us nothing about nurturing our children or loving our spouses. The best it's got is "Honor thy parents" (who have the God-given right to beat children to death if they don't) and "Thou shalt not commit adultery" (unless you're a husband, then you can have sex with multiple women as long as it isn't with another man's wife). The other references to family are Cain-and-Abel-type stories of murder, mayhem and incest that make the characters of the television series, *Desperate Housewives*, look like angelic figures sent from the heavens with the purest of desires and deeds.

In addition, let's not overlook the fact that biblical families were anything but nuclear. In fact, with multiple wives and concubines, such families would be considered not only freaky today, but illegal. Yet, cultural conservatives sell the Judeo-Christian brand of family values based on their beliefs about a book written by imperfect mortals who claimed to have heard divine voices in a violent, pre-enlightened age two thousand years ago. Never mind that today's families and society have little to no resemblance to life back then.

So here we have it, the need to consider *context* when discussing *values*, values that at a different place and time might be considered blessed and sacred, or crude and absurd. Shere Hite, in her book, *Hite Report on the Family*, sums up the contextual forces that influenced the creation of "biblical family values:"

"We are told that the family is a religious and sacred institution, but this is not its origin.

"We tend to forget the family was created in its current form in early patriarchy for political and not religious reasons: *the new political order which would allow lineage and inheritance to pass through men, and not women (as it had previously) had to create a special family. Why? Because it had to solve a special problem, i.e., how could lineage or inheritance flow through men if men do not bear children?*

"The family, a political institution, *was created to solve this dilemma: each man would 'own' a woman who would reproduce for him. Thus laws were set up defining marriage as an institution of male ownership of women and children. Now, each man had to control the sexuality of 'his' woman, for how else could he be sure 'his child' was his?*

"Therefore, restrictions were placed on women's lives and bodies by the early fathers; women's imprisonment in marriage was made a virtue, for example, especially through the later archetype of the meek and self-sacrificing Mary, happy to be of service, never standing up for herself or her own rights...."[54]

I'm not intending a feminist rant here, but to illustrate two important points that we seem to overlook all too often: biblical pronouncements were not all pure, being highly influenced by the vagaries of interpretation, cultural demands, and the politics of canonization; and our Westernized culture bears little resemblance to biblical times. Consequently, the complexion and function of family life has changed as a result, creating a transformed social system whose values have changed as well—in most cases for the better.

Western civilization has advanced from theocratic to aristocratic to democratic forms of government while heightening humanistic principles, particularly the value of equality among people and between the sexes, light years away from a social order based on tribalism, religious fundamentalism and patriarchal hierarchy. Women are not subjugated to serving men, and have moved far beyond hearth and home, fully assimilated into a democratic ownership society. They now own their bodies and own their lives and have available to them all the choices that come with that—to become educated or not, what kind of work to pursue in or out of the home, whether to get married or not, to have children or not.

Today, people marry for love and personal life enhancement, no longer forced into pre-arranged marriages for political alliances between families and countries. And with exponential population growth, procreation isn't necessary for survival. Lastly, medical advances have contributed to significantly longer lifespans, making "till death do you part" a marathon rather than a sprint. The implications of this and all of the cultural shifts that have ensued over the last 2,000 years have created a vastly different world in which Western families live, making context critically important to consider when discussing family life and values.

When pressed to define family values, these so-called "family values advocates" make vague reference to family values being the path of moral superiority as laid out in the Bible, never mentioning the gory and unsavory elements of family life depicted and valued therein. What's promoted is a biblical spin-off, a watered-down version of patriarchy embodied in the so-called "traditional nuclear family structure", a rendering more easily accepted than the flotsam and jetsam of biblical breeding harems.

The tradition they implicitly speak of is obedience to the ultimate authority, God the Father. Families are expected to follow His rules as spoken by the prophets. Through them, we learned of God's commands. And through the fear of His wrath, we are to follow injunctions, to obey as the way of morality.

These moral absolutes, most often involving sexuality, are very comforting, drawing lines in the suburban sand, setting codes of behavior designed to keep eyes from roaming, hormones from raging, and family compositions secure. As the thinking goes, by obeying the rules, suppressing sexuality, and instilling the fear of damnation, we can pass on traditional values to the next generation, be in control of life, of families, of the behaviors of others, and of the big payoff, what happens to us after we die.

This version of biblical family values is an easier sell. Many people can get on board here. No one wants rivals to step into their home, disrupting whatever threads of harmony or illusions of eternal security are there. We all like payoffs and certainty, even if it's a higher authority telling us what to do and how to behave. It's comforting—a throwback to childhood, when the responsibility of tough decisions doesn't exist, when life is black and white and not complicated by shades of gray. But this is not the reality of life—especially in a democracy where freedom reigns and the sound development of personal responsibility constitutes the core of a well-functioning society.

In pointing to the rarely discussed brutality and debauchery embedded within the holy book, and the gaping contextual dissonance between then and now, I argue that today many biblical values are incomprehensible, if not downright obscene. My intention is not to disparage the Bible, but rather to convey the problem with literal interpretations and strict modern-day application. The Bible is one of the most enduring, complex, and mysteriously rich compilations of stories in recorded time. We'd be foolish to not mine its treasures by sifting through the concrete rocks of literalism in order to find the golden nuggets of eternal truths submerged in its symbolism.

But most importantly, the nuggets of wisdom in the Bible aren't truths to be found "out there" in the form of a rulebook or in commandments from on high. They are found in the meanings derived from deep within our hearts. They contain truths that are communicated, felt, and arrived at through our common humanity as Tevye came to learn. These are the immortal messages we need to heed—messages distinct from doctrine, messages devoid of dogmatic and ethnic differences because they lie at the heart and soul of human nature, no matter what religion one subscribes to, or not.

In the following chapters we'll see how the simple, yet profound and transcendent messages of love, empathy, and compassion—basic humanistic principles that involve a higher level of awareness than any concrete, simplistic interpretation of dogma or doctrine can ever provide—are *real* family values. These values are critical for optimum moral development, yet the challenge is to realize them in the most rigorous of soul-testing environments, family life.

5
Religion, Morality and a Sound Society

"The true meaning of religion is thus not simply morality,
but morality touched by emotion."

Matthew Arnold

Religion and morality have become so intertwined in our minds that we tend to consider them one and the same. They're not. We often hear that the Bible sets *the* standard for morality. It doesn't. What *is* true is that moral people live in all corners of the world, religious or not; and *many* religious and cultural roads lead to morality…and don't.

The mistaken belief is that without religion, immorality would overrun society because there would be no moral absolutes to dictate behavior. Yet religious dogmatism has been one of the greatest destroyers of common ground and common good throughout history. Whose god, whose religion, whose absolutes are *The Truth*?

Religious fundamentalists have shown some of the most monstrous forms of inhumanity as witnessed through the jihads, the Crusades and the ongoing battle for holy land where the birthplace of hope for peace on earth has turned into a cesspool of murderous madness. Rather than killing each other over whose absolutes are truth, which peoples are the chosen ones, or whose God is more deserving of reverence, we have to see religion not as an end in itself, but as what it is ultimately intended to be—*a tool to become better human beings by rising to a higher consciousness.*[55]

The way in which this comes about is strikingly different from what conventional wisdom leads us to believe. It requires the hard work of spiritual enlightenment, not the mind-constricting, soul-castrating effects of religious indoctrination. It involves elevating the human spirit with love and compassion, tolerance and forgiveness, not devaluing the human spirit with literal-minded adherence to dogma.

It's crucial to make a distinction between religion as a spiritual quest and religion as doctrine, to broaden our view in order to see universal human truths that can move us closer to a sane, compassionate and cooperative world. Once we do, we might be able to embrace what Einstein referred to as true religion: "True religion is real living; living with all one's soul, with all one's goodness, all one's righteousness."[56] It doesn't get any holier than this.

But along the way, religion has become warped, perverted for political purposes to gain power over the masses by instilling the fear of God. A public that questioned authority, or sought spiritual enlightenment through self-knowledge and personal empowerment were apt to be troublesome. So rulers controlled the populace by promising life everlasting, in exchange for obedience to the moral codes set forth by God. The three major world religions operate from this authoritarian premise, holding patriarchal notions of God the Father delivering commandments from on high, carrying eternal consequences of heavenly rewards or fiery damnation. If you sin, you go to hell. If you're good, you're off to the Promised Land.

The religious right, which promotes "traditional family values," subscribes to this worldview, believing that in order to create a moral society, the fear of God must reign. From this paradigm, the rules about the ways in which children should be raised and family life stabilized have been formed. But what we've learned about character and morality over the last 2,000 years—since the days of stoning women and killing rebellious children—is, dare I say, enlightening.

What *Is* True About the Nature of Morality

Lawrence Kohlberg, an eminent pioneer in moral development research, built on his colleague Jean Piaget's cognitive development model more than fifty years ago, linking stages of moral development to cognitive capacity. His classic model explains that any behavior motivated by the desire to avoid punishment or reap rewards is the most primitive stage of moral development.

Anyone who has spent any amount of time with young children knows that this rather naïve grasp of "right and wrong" is typical for children ages five to eight. Since children at this age have only a budding capacity for abstract reasoning and judgment, rules are interpreted literally and followed obediently. These young children do not have a sophisticated internal conscience that can grasp complex motives, feelings and consequences of behavior beyond their own immediate self-interests. Being "good" is a self-serving enterprise.

When the brain develops in complexity, we gain the ability to "decenter" (see beyond oneself) and come into our full human capacity, progressing through various stages of moral capabilities with the most advanced stage of moral development motivated by grand, overarching humanistic principles, as opposed to concrete rules and simplistic pronouncements of "good" and "bad."

At this pinnacle of moral development, humans are capable of understanding and operating from an interest in the universal rights and needs of others, putting aside self-serving interests. It's a state of being that involves courage, strength of character, and the use of judgment based on one's *inner* moral compass, a solid source of guidance impervious to manipulation by external commandments, pressures, or outside controls.

This reality does not support the claims that religious dogma and authoritarianism instill moral values. In fact, embracing any kind of ideology or submitting to authoritarian rule actually results in the obliteration of personal choice and responsibility because there is no room to think and act in accordance with one's internal moral compass. Standing up for personal truths in the face of power or convention is moral development at its finest. If we want our children to become solid individuals, resilient to peer pressure and the incessant negative influences of our consumer-based, media-saturated, celebrity-hyped, sexually objectified, spiritually devoid culture, we need to support their development, not turn them into obedient sheep.

Right-wing ideology is flat out wrong about the nature of morality. Ironically, those flawed views have been turned back on progressives in the form of righteous rhetoric—the idea that progressives are "morally relativistic." In actuality, the real problem lies in the ways in which the Right reduces humanistic concerns into the simplistic, black-and-white morality of a child on Santa's knee, swearing off naughtiness in the hope of making a killing on Christmas morning.

Inner moral authority in no way means "relativistic" or "hedonistic" as the Right's rhetoric likes to portray it. On the contrary, inner authority requires being grounded in universal moral principles of right and wrong based on our common humanity and interconnectedness. Not reward. Not punishment. It's a moral frame that requires discipline to place selfish desires, ideology and fears aside. It's an empathic approach to morality that lies deep *within* the individual and which requires self-awareness, strength of character, and personal responsibility to evolve into our full human potential. This involves care, concern and empathy for others, which is absolutely critical and impossible to legislate or impose through punishment. It's an inside-out experience that marks the outside-in approach of the religious right woefully misguided and inadequate.

The lack of moral sophistication involving attunement to humanity is precisely the problem we're witnessing in the Republican Party today. There's a shameless absence of character and the human virtues of empathy and compassion, coupled with an overriding concern for selfish interests.

One of the more subtle, yet still frightfully offensive examples of human vacuity came from pro-NRA Jeb Bush whose next-day response to the gun massacre at Umpqua Community College in Oregon where eight students and a professor were randomly and violently murdered in a classroom: "Stuff happens." Stuff? Mass murder is not "stuff." It is a horrific human tragedy. And this "stuff" did not happen in a vacuum. There were victims who lost their lives, families who lost their loved ones, and an entire community who lost their sense of security. If this doesn't demonstrate a disconnection from the soul—his own and that of humanity—I don't know what does.

What Would Jesus Do?

It's quite remarkable that Republicans manage to claim Jesus Christ as their savior, all the while acting in direct opposition to his message. Jesus was on a spiritual mission to bring humanistic values into the soul of the people—new standards based on grace rather than fear, love over law, and forgiveness rather than damnation.

In an ironic twist, the conventional standards Jesus set out to change are the very standards embraced by the Republican Party today. Republicans play on fear, judgment and punishment with their authoritarian worldview, while shirking the humanistic values that Jesus sacrificed his life for, values that are actually part and parcel of democrat ideology.

It was Jesus' rebellion against convention and his progressivism that made him a true evangelical, a "spreader of good news," exemplifying a new vs. traditional path for humanity to follow, overturning old beliefs and codes of behavior along the way. He was the evolutionary model of what human beings can become when they lift themselves to their highest potential, transcending fear and judgment (the sources of sin, or in secular parlance, human fallibility) while embracing grace and forgiveness, love and compassion. He challenged others to find their holy essence through transcendence from fear, not by giving in to fear. *This* is faith in Christ, pure and simple.

Indeed, this glaring deficit is on display among Republicans of every shade these days. There is little true faith in the sense that Jesus preached, grace, or goodwill, much less love for their fellow man—and precious little empathy or compassion. These moral deficiencies are magnified now with an antagonistic, retaliatory, divisive, authoritarian stance on nearly every recent human rights and equality issue. Their responses reek of the very fear and judgment Christ sacrificed his life for.

Interestingly, research has exposed an inconvenient truth: Those who view God as an authoritarian figure are more aggressive and less altruistic than those who do not.[57] We're seeing the influence of fear play out to the hilt today as Republican leaders want to reject asylum for helpless Syrian refugees fleeing unspeakable horror with nowhere to turn because "they" are Muslim, not like "us."

Then we have Republican leaders giving in to the fear of terrorism by waging a "war against Islam" which will not solve terrorism. First, the problem is not Islam, the problem is terrorists who pervert the religion for ideological reasons. Ultimately, this only gives the terrorists what they want—to see the U.S. react to the terror they are instigating. They are baiting the U.S. to fall into an aggressive, anti-Islamic role through the use of fear.

Ted Cruz's threat to carpet-bomb ISIS into oblivion, while provocatively wondering if he could make sand "glow in the dark," is not only evil, arrogant and ignorant, it's just plain stupid. Killing innocent civilians with indiscriminate bombing is a sure-fire way to promote distrust and hatred, create more enemies, and build bad blood between countries for generations to come.

Cruz and the rest of the Republican field have engaged in the lowest form of ethics and leadership imaginable—stoking fear with the calculated use of "the war on terror" for self-serving political gain with potentially dire consequences for the rest of us. This tough guy, "I'll protect America" act promising to "wipe 'em all out," in order to garner votes at the expense of greater human interest, is anti-American, anti-religious and scummy. There's a lot of sinning in the form of fear-mongering and judgment going on in the Republican Party, and very little transcendence through love and compassion. Sorry fellas. This is *not* faith in Christ.

Republicans have turned away from the moral message Jesus surrendered his life for, and are bastardizing Christianity just as Middle East terrorists are bastardizing Islam—meaning is interpreted and passages are selected, then twisted, for egomaniacal purposes. As Shakespeare's character Shylock from the *Merchant of Venice* opines: "The devil can cite scripture for his purpose."[58]

Biblical interpretations are often used as poorly conceived rationalizations to do, say and believe, whatever the hell one wants. In these instances, scripture is usually tainted with reasons to fear the "non-believers," effective for rallying ideological followers. Whenever an "us vs. them" dichotomy is wielded along with a lack of empathy and compassion, you know that religion, "the goal of which is to become a better human being," is being grotesquely misused.

The jig is up, Repubs. Put your weapon—err, Bible—down. Put your hands up and slowly step away from the pulpit.

The Ultimate Moral Yardstick

With the merging of cultures and races so prevalent today, finding the fundamental principles and universal truths that transcend the conventions of any particular society or religion allows us to determine bottom line moral standards. Whether we turn to Christianity or any of the other major world religions, we'll find the same nugget of "truth," once all the fundamentalist dogma is scraped away. The common denominator across all religions, and even among non-secular humanitarians, is the Golden Rule. No imposing figure in the sky threatening eternal damnation is needed. Aline D. Wolfe in her book, *Nurturing the Spirit*, listed the passages from various religions that point to the Golden Rule as a guiding principle:

Buddhism: "Hurt not others in ways that you yourself would find hurtful."

Hinduism: "Do not unto others what would cause you pain if done to you."

Judaism: "What is hateful to you, do not do to others."

Taoism:	"Regard your neighbor's gain as your own gain and your neighbor's loss as your own loss."
Christianity:	"Do unto others as you would have them do unto you."
Islam:	"None of you is a believer until he desires for his brother that which he desires for himself." [59]

The Golden Rule requires a connection to the humanity of each other that translates into moral and ethical behavior guided by the "do unto others" principle, simple in concept yet epically difficult to heed. In order to follow the Golden Rule, three aspects of moral behavior—thoughts, feelings and actions—need to be in alignment.

Complementing Kohlberg's cognitive model of moral development that underscores the importance of justice, is Martin Hoffman's work over the last four decades that focuses on the emotional component of morality—empathy. While justice is a cognitive concept that resides in the head, empathy is its counterpart, a feeling that resides in the heart. It is a connection to other people, to our communities, and to humanity that in turn connects us to ourselves and makes us want to do right by others. Hoffman refers to empathy as "the spark of human concern for others, the glue that makes social life possible."[60]

Empathy is the ability to "feel with" another person, to take the emotional and cognitive perspective of others while remaining present to our own inner wisdom and emotional experience.

I see it as the moral juice that compels us toward justice, virtue and goodwill. It involves an awareness of the impact our behavior has on another so that our conscience can serve us, and others, in a just, humane, spiritually enlightened way.

It doesn't take an advanced degree in theology or social sciences to see that empathy, which is the gateway to compassion, is humanity's essential goodness, the ability to care—to feel with and for other living beings. It explains why people can be moral anywhere in the world, no matter what religious text they do or do not follow. And it explains what propelled the moral courage we witnessed on 9/11 when individuals risked their lives in an effort to save people they did not even know—empathic, compassionate and courageous people who ran up towers that were burning to the ground, and who wrestled hijackers mid-flight so that another target of innocents would be spared. These moral heroes defy pigeonholing by race or creed or otherwise—straight and gay, religious and secular, Christian and Muslim, Jewish and Hindu. Morality lives deeper than religious beliefs of right or wrong, of my god, or your god, or no god. Morality comes from the heart and lives in the soul, not the head.

While "goodness" comes through our connection to others, it stands to reason that "evil" may be utter lack of connection. In studying violent and abusive people, researchers have identified a "psychological fault line," which is an apparent lack of empathy. Terrorists and torturers have described how they learned to dissociate from the feelings of their victims in order to do their "jobs."[61] Think Timothy McVeigh when he chillingly referred to the babies he blew up in his 1995 Oklahoma City bombing as "collateral damage." This type of perverse disconnection explains how even the fervently religious can be immoral in spite of their sanctimonious beliefs. There was no way in heaven or hell that McVeigh or Bin Laden's hit men could have committed their brutal massacres if they had an ounce of empathy and compassion for the suffering inflicted on the victims and their families. Empathy—being "one with" another—means that hurting another hurts oneself. And compassion—love, care and concern—makes victimizing another impossible.

Whether we're talking about delusional hijackers flying jets into skyscrapers filled with innocent people, predatory lenders whose underhanded actions lead to the financial ruin of countless Americans and spark a nationwide housing crisis, or sneaky spouses betraying their partners' trust, the ability to be fully aware—in body, mind and soul—of the impact your actions have on another, and *care*, is a crucial guide for determining moral behavior. This is when hurting or doing wrong to someone else is so painful and/or distressing to oneself, it outweighs whatever tempting rewards would be associated with the crime, hedonistic pursuit, or self-serving action.

And finally, in addition to a sense of justice (cognition) and empathy (feeling), the third leg of the triad comprising a solid moral foundation is behavior. The actions one takes or doesn't take require discipline, self-control and the management of emotions. Summarizing conclusions drawn from his decades of research, Daniel Goleman states in his book *Emotional Intelligence*,

> *"There is growing evidence that fundamental ethical stances in life stem from underlying emotional capacities...Those who*

are at the mercy of their impulse—who lack self-control—suffer
a moral deficiency: The ability to control impulse is the base of
will and character. By the same token, the root of altruism lies
in empathy, the ability to read emotions in others: lacking a
sense of another's need or despair, there is no caring."[62]

What's needed for self-discipline is the integration of both the emotional and rational centers of the brain so that choices about moral behavior can be made. This type of integration allows for integrity of character that is ultimately expressed through behavior that's in alignment with rightful values and beliefs. What must be brought to the table is not only clear-headed logic, but also connection to ourselves and others in the form of empathy and compassion. This allows us to step outside of ourselves to see and feel the impact our behaviors will have on another, thus making it possible for us to translate the "do unto others" rule into principled action.

Most of us agree in principle with the Golden Rule. Yet, there remains a great disagreement: *What ensures these moral capabilities? The Bible? The Torah? The Koran?* Conservative Supreme Court justices? Cosmic energy? *And how do we instill these qualities in our children?* Is it Sunday school? A rod well used on an otherwise spoiled child? Heterosexual parents? DNA? Dumb luck?

Angel Lobes and the Devil's Back Alley

With advances in brain scan technology over the last couple of decades, neuroscientists have been able to uncover fascinating facts about the brain and its relationship to behavior, supporting "softer" social science research that's been difficult to quantify. It's become increasingly clear that the capacity for moral behavior lies within the structure and function of the brain. If the brain hasn't developed properly, an unhealthy character will result.

While many areas of the brain are involved in any given function, two areas are of particular note here—the "angel lobes" and the "devil's back alley", references to moral capacities, or lack thereof. On a very basic level, angel lobes are the prefrontal lobes considered to be the higher brain (a.k.a. prefrontal cortex or PFC). This area of the brain guides thought, action and emotion. The prefrontal cortex makes abstract reasoning, sound judgment, and impulse control possible, as well as the ability to feel empathy, guilt or remorse—all necessary for healthy character and moral behavior. Often referred to as "conscience," these abilities allow us to rise above our basest instincts to make executive decisions about how to behave. Because of this function, the prefrontal cortex has been deemed the seat of our character, "the CEO of the soul."[63]

As anyone who has ever flown into a testy snit can testify, even the best of us are not always operating with our rational brain fully engaged. At these times we're reacting rather than responding; our actions are based on pure emotion before our thoughts even have a chance to get involved. The "higher brain" appears to be out to lunch. How does this happen and what do we need to do to bring our prefrontal cortex back online?

Brain scientist Joseph LeDoux has been able to explain this phenomenon by identifying two avenues in the brain for processing emotion—the "low road" (a.k.a. the devil's back alley) that bypasses the cortex altogether by way of a small almond-shaped structure called the amygdala, and the "high road" where the angel lobes of the prefrontal cortex become involved, tempering emotion with thought or mindful self-awareness. The amygdala is believed to store emotional impressions and unconscious memories capable of activating a fight-or-flight reaction before the rational brain even knows what's going on. It's a shortcut triggered by fear (rational or irrational, conscious or unconscious) that evolved to help us survive under threatening circumstances. It's why you jump when a shadowy figure appears out of the darkness, though on second look it is clearly the friend you were expecting to meet.

While instinctive reactions can be useful, they can also get us into a heap of trouble when rational thought is called for, hence the term "devil's back alley."[64] Daniel Goleman refers to this phenomenon as an "emotional hijack," aptly named because emotions take over, rendering us captive to our "lower" selves. Emotional hijacking is what's going on whenever we're reacting rather than responding. Reactivity of this sort is most common with those closest to us—our children and spouses—which makes managing emotions in family life so challenging. And emotional hijacking is precisely what Republicans are doing when they use fear-inciting rhetoric for political persuasion. Peddling along the low road like there is no tomorrow, they tap into fear, eliciting emotions and primitive instinct to move their campaigns forward, as opposed to reason.

Interestingly, research has demonstrated structural differences in the brain that make conservatives more susceptible to fear-based reactions. Brain scan technology has revealed a larger right amygdala (the fear and anxiety center) among conservatives, which accounts for the authoritarian personality characteristics discussed in Chapter 1 (i.e., need for control, fear of differences leading to bigotry, black-and-white thinking, and rigid rules in attempt to handle uncertainty that creates anxiety, etc.). Liberals, on the other hand, were found to have a larger anterior cingulate cortex, which functions like a clutch allowing one to more easily process emotions and shift from fear to rationality. Along with this comes cognitive flexibility and characteristics such as optimism, openness to new experiences, people, belief systems, etc. that make up the liberal mindset that is more "go with the flow."[65]

Having leaders and politicians who are operating from the low road portends trouble. Unless true survival needs are being met, low-road behaviors can be highly maladaptive as we unconsciously react vs. consciously and conscientiously respond to whatever it is we're faced with—be it challenges, problems, conflicts, whims, desires, political discourse, philosophical disagreement, etc. No matter who you are—policeman, politician, pundit, or parent—if your amygdala is reactively running the show when it is not a life or death survival need, it's generally a compromised response. Sound decisions, effective coping strategies, productive analysis, compassionate parenting, or wise and virtuous leadership require involvement with the higher centers of our brain.

On the high road all parts of the brain are working in an integrated fashion, giving a person response flexibility,[66] akin to hitting a pause button and being able to choose how to respond (vs. react) in the midst of a flood of emotions or competing desires. Neurological connectivity in the prefrontal cortex allows for simultaneous awareness of self (i.e., thoughts, feelings, impulses, and desires) of others (empathy and perspective taking) and rational consideration of possible responses. It's what's happening in your brain, for example, when you "bite your tongue" or when acting in any number of gracious ways that involves gaining control of emotion. Sounds a lot like Jesus' call for enlightenment by transcending fear in order to act with love and compassion, calling upon humankind to get those angel lobes in gear.

This is not to say that emotions and desires are the scourge of our existence and we should ignore them, deny them, or suppress them, which is the tendency of the traditional, authoritarian approach to morality. Again, there's a need for the *integration* of both the emotional and rational centers of the brain. It's not surprising that without our rational brain engaged, we're at the mercy of our impulses and emotions. What is surprising is that the reverse is true as well: we need access to our emotional world in order to be rational. People with brain damage to the frontal lobe (the emotional control center and the seat of personality) are severely limited in their ability to plan, make decisions, and take another's perspective.[67] In other words, emotions provide our rational mind with important information needed to make sense of our world, think things through and carry out logical tasks.

So, it's not the repression of feelings or denial of their existence; it's the use of feelings and emotions as important information. This brings not only clear-headed logic to the table, but also connection to ourselves and others in the form of empathy and compassion, allowing us to step outside of ourselves to see and feel the impact our behaviors will have on another, thus making it possible for us to translate the "do unto others" rule into principled action.

The quote at the start of this chapter from the 19th Century philosopher and cultural critic Matthew Arnold reflected the importance of emotion as it applies to morality: "The true meaning of religion is thus not simply morality, but morality touched by emotion." And 21st Century neuroscientist Antonio Damasio corroborates this claim with high-tech findings suggesting that morality takes hold in the rich emotional circuitry in the brain.[68]

When touched by emotion, religion becomes more than a set of rules; it involves connecting with the human heart. Looking at the common themes present in religion and spirituality, including the Golden Rule, this feeling is a sense of oneness, unity, or connectedness to others through empathy and compassion. When we feel this, which is a form of love acknowledged by all religions (*agape* in Latin, *chesed* in Hebrew and *ishq* in Arabic) and humanists alike, the desire to do right transcends fear and the darker elements of human nature.

As becomes clear, morality doesn't depend upon religion, but upon the appropriate development of the brain allowing for emotional, social and spiritual resonance. Morality grows from the inside out, rooted in personal experience and in connection to others. As we explored above, it involves being able to shift out of the more primitive fear-based circuitry in the brain, to a more evolved, higher state where thoughts and feelings are integrated into our awareness. Overriding fear and other emotions in service of a greater purpose is the ultimate challenge that is both the blessing and burden of being human.

The ability to love while tempering fear and other base emotions is the hallmark of a spiritually advanced person and is the making of a truly sound society. Culture wars, the goal of which is to make biblical law the rule of law, will never enhance our society because the focus is on trying to repress "the bad." Repression never fixes anything.

In addition, what these warriors have deemed "the bad" is not the problem. The only way to enhance our culture's moral values is by developing the character of those within the culture via emotional and spiritual development. While it may be easier to wage a cultural war that focuses on the personal values, beliefs and actions of others than it is to come face to face with the flaws and shadows of our own character, there is no other way. It begins with each of us.

6
Building Character
From the Inside Out

"The finest qualities of our nature, like the bloom on fruits,
can be preserved only by the most delicate handling."

Henry David Thoreau

Whenever discussing character and morality, it's assumed that traditional family values play a key role—some mythical, wholesome quality of family life that magically translates into raising "good" children. Family life *is* key; research on child and moral development points to parenting and family relations as crucial influences from nearly every conceivable angle. What the research does *not* suggest, however, is that traditional family values, code for the Bible-based child-rearing philosophy espoused by the religious right, promote the highest forms of character and moral development. In fact, the opposite may be true.

Let's examine the facts that challenge this conventional wisdom. We'll look at what experts have to say about nurturing optimal development in our children—the nuances of parenting styles and the quality of parent–child relations. We'll come to see why traditional family values and their authoritarian influences hinder development with outside-in attempts to control through obedience, and why the use of shame and other harmful measures ultimately create a fragile sense of self and splinter the soul. We'll then see how an inside-out approach of childrearing through empathic attunement and intimate connection nurtures soulful, sound character development, underpinning moral behavior.

Parenting and Brain Development

Building upon the burgeoning field of brain neuroscience, a subfield known as interpersonal neurobiology, which studies the interface of interpersonal relationships and brain development, has received much attention over the last couple of decades. Evidence suggests that the brain develops in a relational context and is experience dependent, whereby "human connections create neuronal connections."[69] Simply put, the growth and development of the brain is dependent upon social interactions, especially attachment bonds early in life.

Most of us easily intuit and would readily agree that parents wield an enormous influence on a child's emotional, psychological and character development. Numerous theories since the time of Freud have suggested as much. With brain-scan technology we now have ways to peer into the brain to get quantifiable information that illuminates what's actually happening as development unfolds.

The hard data of brain neuroscience—which areas of the brain are lighting up with activity, the growth and relative size of the various structures, the strength of neuronal connections, and the neurochemical byproducts released when bonding through empathy occurs (or doesn't occur)—support classic psychological theories of bonding and attachment, which emphasize the critical impact this first intimate relationship has on psychological development.[70, 71] These findings correlate with classic parenting research as well, pointing to the immense significance the emotional quality of parent–child interactions has on social/emotional functioning and development of self.[72]

Attachment bonds are at root a neuro-biochemical process with a built-in reward system that releases the body's natural opiates when an empathic connection is made between parent and infant. When an infant cries in distress and the attuned caretaker sensitively responds, an emotional communication takes place that can be described as "feeling felt." This emotional resonance releases soothing, pleasurable neurotransmitters, relieving distress on a deep physiological level, acting as neuromodulators in the nervous system.[73]

Attachment bonds are also "necessary for neuronal activity in the cerebral cortex."[74] In other words, optimal brain functioning and development of brain circuitry requires the chemical bath that's released during bonding, making brain development dependent upon empathic attunement. This is especially true in the prefrontal brain regions that regulate and process social emotions such as empathy. In a very literal sense, empathy begets empathy. The desire to connect interpersonally as well as the capacity for empathy and moral behavior are born from the neuro-biochemical effects attachment bonds.

Empathic attunement meets the infant's innate need for emotional connection on a psychological dimension as well. When an infant/baby/child's physical and emotional needs are perceived by caretakers and sensitively responded to, a sense of security is internalized. They learn that they can reach out and receive what they need—intimate connection, followed by caretaking that satisfies their desires. From this they learn that they are effective in getting their needs met (mastery and confidence), that they are valued and loved, that their feelings matter, and that others can be relied upon for care and comfort—all of this leading to the development of trust. These experiences create a secure attachment, influencing the child's sense of self and the blueprints for intimate relationships carried into adulthood.

Unfortunately, the conventional wisdom coming from family values advocates narrowly dictates that children need a mother and a father (without recognizing the *quality* of this bond) and anything other than that spells a lifetime of trouble. Given what we now know about the brain and psychological development, it's time for conventional wisdom to reflect the truth about what really matters: Children need empathically connected and caring adults in their lives to shepherd them into adulthood. It's the emotional *quality* of the relationship that is important—empathic, loving, stable and consistent—not sexual orientation, traditional roles, nor a "religious" upbringing. Empathy is empathy. Emotional attunement is emotional attunement. Love is love. And without this, children are harmed.

It's easy to imagine what empathically attuned caregiving would look like between a parent and baby. A fussy baby needs something—to be held, relieved of gas, fed, a diaper changed—and the parent seems to almost instinctively respond. A baby's needs are fairly basic—they either need stimulation or relief from some form of discomfort—and they let you know about it, loud and clear. It's hard to miss the cue that a baby needs an attuned response from their caretaker. When the caretaker responds, the baby rewards them by now being content and no longer crying!

But as babies grow into toddlers and older children, a parent's lack of emotional attunement becomes more common because needs, especially emotional needs, can be more nuanced, complex and difficult to perceive. In fact, many "normal" and traditional parenting practices are unwittingly dismissive of a child's emotional state, which is hugely problematic because the need for emotional connection, resonance, and feel-good opiates does not end in infancy. It's a need that continues throughout the lifespan and is especially critical for the still developing child who looks to their caretakers for validation, love, containment, and guidance.

Loving, sensitive attunement that validates a child's internal experience is paramount not only because of the physiological need for soothing. Attuned interaction that identifies and responds to the child's emotional states teaches them how to identify their emotions, make sense of them, and bring them under control.

Parents also serve as mirrors reflecting back to children who they are and what they are experiencing, powerfully determining the child's sense of self. If their emotions (especially the overwhelming kind) are routinely not acknowledged or responded to by the all-important love object (parent/caretaker), the child fails to integrate these emotions, compromising what's called ego integration or a solid sense of self. We'll explore this and the impact on character development more as we turn to research on various parenting styles.

A Parenting Style That Works

There has been consistent evidence over the years that good parenting boils down to three basic qualities: 1) acceptance and warmth, 2) discipline (as distinct from punishment), and 3) support of the child's budding autonomy. While discipline is readily understood as important, the emotional tenor of the parent–child relationship (acceptance and warmth, support of autonomy) often goes unrecognized in the everyday interactions of parents with their children. Yet, emotional interactions are absorbed and play a formidable role in the formation of a child's identity and adjustment, similar in concept to imprinting. Just as discipline shapes a child's behavior, a child's sense of him or herself is shaped by the emotional messages conveyed, both overtly and covertly.

Developmental psychologist Diana Baumrind's parenting research in the 1960's has become a classic in the field, having produced a parenting typology that is still used today. She identified four basic parenting styles and an optimal approach to parenting based on widely accepted principles. Without going into the minute details regarding the dimensions of classification, I will simply describe the four parenting styles, then get to the heart of what is considered ideal, what isn't, and why.

Four Types of Parenting Styles

1. **Authoritative**—Authoritative parents are openly affectionate and highly responsive to the child's emotional and physical needs. They shape their child's behavior through a process called induction, which is firm limit setting along with explanation and discussion. Appropriate consequences are used in a just and consistent way. There is two-way communication with the child, whose feelings and opinions are openly received and treated as valid and valuable. Communication and expectations are clear. In short, it's a warm and positive emotional climate with firm discipline, respectful of the child. Children from these types of parents tend to be adaptable, competent, and achievement oriented. They have good social skills and peer acceptance with a low level of antisocial or aggressive behavior. Overall, they have a positive sense of self and a sound capacity for self-regulation.

2. **Authoritarian**—Authoritarian parents express less affection, are less tuned in to the feeling states of their children, and use punishment by asserting power or withdrawing love. This type of parent values obedience over independence, can be unnecessarily controlling and restrictive, and does not encourage the expression of individuality or assertiveness. Communication is typically a one-way street, and conformity is the aim. Physical or emotional punishment such as shame or humiliation is often used, and the emotional climate typically runs from cool to outright negative. This old-school parenting model

encapsulates traditional family values, and is no longer considered the ideal way to parent. Children from these families are more likely to be irritable and conflicted, showing signs of both anxiety and anger. They tend to be conforming under the thumb of authority figures, but lack self-guidance, are not socially skillful, are susceptible to being bullied and tend to have low self-esteem.

3. **Permissive**—Permissive parents are filled with warmth and acceptance but fail to set limits. This style of parenting essentially accepts all behavior with no discernment, consistent rules, limits or discipline. It's the parent who allows their child to draw on walls with color markers because "they are expressing themselves," or the parent who gives in to their child's tantrums instead of putting the kibosh on whining or screaming. Children from these families fail to be properly socialized, showing uncontrolled, impulsive behavior with low levels of self-regulation and self-reliance.

4. **Neglectful-Uninvolved**—This parenting style is missing both warmth and limit setting. There is little to no nurturing or affection with a complete absence of rules, limits and discipline, although there may be harsh and random punishment. These children are essentially raising themselves, lacking connection and any kind of human reference point for learning, with the possible exception of random and volatile interventions by a parent who's "had it." Children from these families tend to be underdeveloped on many levels due to extreme neglect. They're often impulsive with little to no coping

skills, either externalizing problems (aggressiveness) or internalizing problems (depression), with low self-esteem and low capacity for self-regulation.

(Note: Baumrind's model uses the term "demandingness" as one of the critical dimensions for assessing quality of parenting. In my view, it is a poorly chosen term with vague and negative connotations. I would prefer to describe this dimension as "limit setting." What she is actually referring to is not the type of demandingness that exerts psychological control and consequently intrudes on emotional development. Rather, it supports development with firm expectations about behavior.)

Of the four above categories, there is little doubt or disagreement that permissive and neglectful parenting styles are harmful to a child's growth and development. The controversy between authoritarian and authoritative parenting styles lies in the differences in how a person views: 1) the role of a parent, 2) the nature of children, and 3) the elements of raising a "good child."

Old-school attitudes such as: "Children should be seen and not heard," "I'll give you something to cry about," "No child of mine is going to—" have traditionally been seen as the right way to parent. This authoritarian parenting style stems from patriarchal, biblical beliefs that children are born inherently bad or immoral. Thus, it's the parent's job is to "break the will" of the child. In this parenting paradigm, "good" children obey and show deference to a looming parent figure.

With authoritative parenting, on the other hand, the role of the parent is to develop the good in children rather than beat or otherwise attempt to force the bad out of them. There is no sinful spirit that needs to be squelched. Children are similar to diamonds in the rough—inherently precious, yet needing refinement. The good is brought forth through love, guidance and firm discipline.

While family values advocates cling to authoritarian parenting practices as the right way, authoritative parenting has been deemed the ideal parenting style in a wide range of research. As we can see from the descriptive list above, authoritative parenting essentially involves empathic attunement, even though it's not identified as such. Consideration for the child's feelings, open communication, curiosity about motivations for wrong behavior, and respect, etc. are all forms of empathic attunement that nurture the budding individuality of the child.

Engaging with children empathically, setting firm limits, and discussing with them the consequences of their behavior (such as, how another might feel, why something might be dangerous, or why a given rule is in place, etc.), gives them the ability to put themselves in someone else's shoes. When parents engage in this style of parenting, they are fortifying the structure and function of the child's prefrontal cortex, essentially lending their prefrontal cortex to the child while theirs is developing. The neurological connections being made integrates the emotional brain with the thinking brain, allowing for the tempering of emotions and along with it, the ability to rein in impulses and unacceptable behavior.

Empathic attunement is a critically positive experience for the child not only because it supports neurological development, but also because it speaks to the *humanity* of the child—they are esteemed and their feelings are regarded with respect. Contrary to what authoritarian parents fear, this is not spoiling a child.

Nor will the child become morally soft. Valuing a child and their emotional experiences *while holding them to high standards of behavior appropriate for their age* is the best thing a parent can do to foster optimal development.

While the authoritarian parenting philosophy of past generations has been falling away, new problems have arisen due to a lack of understanding of what children actually need. In many cases, the pendulum has swung in the opposite direction—from overly controlling and dismissive to indulgent and too permissive. Allow me to stress that being sensitive and loving toward one's child does not mean limitless indulgence or meaningless doting. Rather, it's the type of love that acknowledges the child's feelings and honors their autonomy while being firm with expectations about behavior. This is the type of nurturing that gives sustenance to the soul.

The human equality to which I refer here is very different than equality of power. Parents are clearly in charge, making the rules and setting appropriate limits with consequences. The difference is that the position of power is not being misused, rather is used judiciously and graciously. This parenting ideal is reminiscent of the Buddhist ideal of the enlightened person whose *words are clear, but never harsh.*[75] When children are compassionately guided, they learn to be cooperative with a solid respect for themselves and others. There's not much more a parent could ask for.

This view of parenting is not yet fully assimilated into our cultural norm, as displayed recently by 2016 presidential candidate, Ted Cruz. In attempting to make a sanctimonious point about truth telling in his campaign, he proudly used as an example: "In my house, if my daughter Catherine, the five-year-old, says something she knows to be false, she gets a spanking." How ignorant of him to think that this is something to boast about. Yet, far too many righteously believe that this type of punishment, or indeed, any type of punishment, makes children moral or teaches them a valuable lesson.

It makes children many things, but being moral is not one of them. It makes them angry and resentful. (Curiously enough, during television footage on the campaign trail, we witnessed Cruz's older daughter refuse to kiss him and run in the opposite direction whenever he attempted to draw her near.) It makes them reactively rebellious or passively obedient, neither of which is psychologically healthy. It makes them feel badly about themselves, which is different than feeling badly about their behavior.

Being hit, or spanked as people like to euphemize, tells the child that they are *not* worthy of loving and respectful treatment; their personal boundaries can be violated by anyone with more power; and doing something bad means they *are* bad, and thus, deserving of harm and mistreatment. All of these messages objectify the child. From the paradigm where being good means being obedient (which is different than being cooperative), submission becomes more important than the child's feelings and their relationship. This becomes a big problem.

Spanking and other kinds of sanctified maltreatment irreparably damage the bond of trust, admiration and love the child needs and wants to have for their parent. Paradoxically, punishment does not increase the desire for, or likelihood of, future cooperation. In fact, authoritarian parenting practices are a repeatedly documented risk factor for antisocial behavior.

Related to this is Martin Hoffman's work on empathy where he has found that "empathic morality can be disrupted by power assertive childrearing and other harsh cultural practices..."[76] A multitude of studies suggest that authoritarian parenting may limit empathic development[77] and can foster aggressive behavior.[78] No surprise here, aggressive control tactics give rise to aggressive behavior. If parents want to encourage positive, kind, well-mannered behavior, they need to be positive, kind and well mannered toward their children. This means parenting with empathy, kindness, and warmth along with firm limit setting. Once again, decades of research meets common sense.

Punishment vs. Discipline

This brings me to the typically unrecognized point that must be highlighted: *There is an essential difference between punishment and discipline.* Although they are often seen as one and the same, they are not. Punishment demands; discipline guides. Punishment imposes obedience; discipline instills values. Punishment teaches that those who have power can force others to obey through punitive measures or the manipulative use of fear; discipline inspires cooperation.

The outside-in approach of punishment results in behaviors and actions that may result in obedience but are not rooted in empathy and personal values. This type of morality can be seen as a superficial overlay, easily cracked, often resulting in the all-too-common hypocrisy found among the morally righteous. Discipline, on the other hand, is an inside-out approach that provides an inner moral compass through nurturing relationships, dialogue, example and natural, appropriate consequences. Here, morality is internalized through meaningful lessons that touch the soul. There's a desire to do right because it *feels* right—it's in alignment with one's sense of self and personal values.

This is the story of Christ and his disciples. His goal was to bring love and mercy into hearts, not blind obedience empty of soul. There was nothing authoritarian about Jesus; he didn't force anyone to follow in his footsteps, smacking them around when their behavior was less than enlightened. His disciples observed his teachings because of love and admiration for him, not fear of him. And he gained love and admiration by showing love and admiration. It was Christ's *grace* that made him the potent conduit that he was, sharing his message of love and compassion, values that were readily absorbed because hearts were open in his presence, by his example and what he gave of himself.

Punishment, on the other hand, is a form of institutionalized mistreatment that does the exact opposite; it damages the relationship between parent and child. Belittling, breaking the will, trampling on the spirit, shame and humiliation, either verbally or through physical punishment, are assaults on the personhood of another that may be effective for controlling behavior in the short term, but do nothing for establishing internalization of morals and values.

When under assault, any person naturally pulls away and closes down to protect themselves, making learning impossible and the attempt to teach a lesson a lost cause. The child also loses respect for vindictive parents who have become poor role models incapable of good judgment, impulse control, and empathic relating. And lastly, a child will instinctively feel fear, anger, resentment, and even rage (usually bottled up due to fear) toward the punisher who is aggressively crossing the victim's personal boundaries—not an effective way to inspire the desire to cooperate or teach a child about love and relationships.

Fundamentally, punishment is about force of will and emotional assault, sometimes physical. It's a hostile action driven by emotions. Those who inflict punishment will deny this. "It's for your own good" is their glib rationalization. Granted, the punisher may be in a state of disassociation, so they may not be aware of their hostile emotions, maybe even completely numb. But one thing is certain: The harshly punitive parent is absolutely *not* feeling love and compassion in that moment. No one could hit, shame, or humiliate another if they were feeling care and concern, empathy and compassion. Punishment as described here is about the discharge of vengeful emotions. It is not about love or logic, or even teaching a lesson. There are effective ways to teach good behavior; punishment is not one of them. It only serves to give the one with power a feeling of control.

When a parent is empathically connected to their child with care and concern, love and compassion, they're interested in what compelled the bad behavior and what they can do to help the child. They would attempt to understand, to let them know they are loved even though their behavior was wrong or hurtful, disappointing or enraging. Punishing a child does just the opposite. The message that's sent is that the child is not loveable, that they are bad, and then they behave as if they are bad and unlovable. Labels precede children; they live up to, or down to, the expectations others have of them.

Research on moral identity, which studies how self-concept relates to moral behavior, supports this. Findings suggest that individuals are motivated to make choices that are consistent with their sense of self.[79] It's also been suggested that moral identity may account for the common disconnection between knowing what's right and doing what's right.[80] In other words, if a person views themselves as bad, they are likely to act badly in spite of knowing better.

We have a lot of information here that shows just how backward an authoritarian approach to childrearing really is. If we want to raise sound, moral children, we need to shift away from punishment to discipline, away from authoritarian parenting practices to authoritative practices, away from patriarchal, traditional family values to more enlightened humanistic values that nurture the soul.

Children really need very little beyond empathic attunement, parental guidance and limits, and support of their budding individuality. Yet, this little need is hugely demanding because it requires parents to dig deep and find grace at the most challenging times—times when we'd like nothing more than to just hogtie our children, toss them into a soundproof room, and let them have a good long think about their misbehavior. It's a daunting task to be a loving role model and not let our frustration and anger splay all over the place. We have to regulate our own emotions; otherwise, we can't teach children to regulate theirs. We have to be judicious with our power—when it needs to be exerted and how—and resist using this power in a negative way lest we damage our children in ways we do not intend.

Contrary to attitudes embedded in traditional family values, a "willful" child is a good thing, something that will likely get them through challenging times in life. The trick is to honor that spirit while encouraging the child's natural desire to cooperate and please, to feel love, pride and acceptance from, and for, their parents. Again, it's the quality of relationship—not demands and commands, or shallow praise and scorching punishment—that nurtures moral development and allows children to grow and glow from the inside out.

The Toxic Effects of Shame

We can't address morals without mentioning shame, which is often used in a misguided attempt to teach moral behavior. Not only does it not work, it results in some unfavorable consequences. While guilt and shame are often used interchangeably, they're not one and the same. Shame is about character—who one is. Guilt is about behavior—what one has done. ("I am ashamed of myself" vs. "I feel guilty about doing that"). Guilt is redeemable. Shame isn't. It's an emotion that implicates the core of one's being.

While shame, like guilt, is a social emotion that helps conscience develop, there is a big difference between the natural feeling of shame that arises when one might not live up to personal standards and values, and the toxic experience brought about by shaming with contempt, rejection and withdrawal of love that kills the spirit and damages the soul. The former is a relatively tolerable experience, a feeling that serves as a self-correcting measure, essentially the opposite of pride. The latter is a vicious assault involving one's personhood.

To get at the difference, imagine this: The first experience is similar to a child touching a hot stove, getting burned, and learning that it's hot. The second is a parent taking a child's hand and holding it on a hot burner to teach them it's hot. One is a natural lesson learned. The other is a lesson inflicted on a child treated as an object whose feelings don't matter. Suddenly, it's a soul-searing experience, a lesson about much more than a hot stove. It's about self/other, trust/fear, love/hate, compassion/cruelty, empathic attunement/utter disconnection and thorough emotional abandonment.

Developmental psychologists suggest that the experience of being shamed as a matter of course (made to feel bad, dirty, insignificant, unworthy, unlovable, etc.) is a relational trauma with far-reaching effects on body, mind and soul. Shame-induced ruptures in the attachment bond have been named "little t" traumas because these experiences register as a literal trauma to the system, releasing stress hormones that interfere with the processing and integration of emotions, very similar in nature to post traumatic stress disorder. The "little t" refers to the fact that these experiences are often passed off as normal in the sense they are not seen as traumatic the way that catastrophic events are, yet are psychologically damaging nonetheless, especially when repeatedly inflicted, putting one in a constant state of psychological stress.

Just as we are hardwired to bond for survival purposes, we are hardwired to panic when attachment bonds are harshly broken either through explicit attempts to shame or implicitly by withdrawal of love and emotional rejection. In response to this psychological assault, a cascade of stress hormones triggers a fight-or-flight response with a surge of adrenaline, racing heart, constriction in the gut, paling or flushing of the face, etc. The stress hormone cortisol that's released interferes with the ability to make neurological connections, which not only compromises the ability to process emotions, it also compromises the ability to learn. This makes shame ineffective on a physiological level for teaching any kind of lesson.

On a psychological level, stress arises from fear for one's emotional safety and constitution of self. In his book, *Soul Murder*, Leonard Shengold considers shaming to be murder of the soul, where shaming is explained as the deliberate attempt to eradicate or compromise the separate identity of another person. To be mortified is nothing less than the "mort" (the Latin root meaning the "death") of the soul.[81]

Indeed, shaming is the exact opposite of soul-nourishing, loving intimacy, which is why eyes avert when someone feels ashamed—the impulse is to hide rather than be exposed in an emotionally threatening situation. While love prompts the secretion of naturally occurring opioids and oxytocin, amplifying highly pleasurable feelings (connection, safety, comfort and joy), rejection or withdrawal of love can be devastatingly painful. Physiologically, there is a plunge in the brain's feel-good chemicals much like a drug withdrawal, bringing about physical symptoms such as a hollow emptiness, a tightening in the pit of the stomach, and literal ache in the heart. Many of us know how shattering it can be to experience rejection by a love partner as an adult, even when shaming is not involved. Add shaming to the loss of love, and even more trauma is inflicted on an even more vulnerable person whose sense of self is not yet formed.

We would do well if we could remember this one simple point as a parenting strategy: To handle hearts delicately and preciously, like the bloom of a fruit, while standing firm in expectations about behavior. From this, children feel cherished while learning to be cooperative. And from this, they learn to value themselves and others, not a better foundation on which to grow character. What we see and believe about our children is what our children see and believe about themselves.

This is precisely why parents carry such a huge responsibility, a responsibility that is rarely in the forefront of our consciousness, but needs to be. Parenting is not just about getting children to behave, have manners, be good students, or even be kind to others. It's also about helping our children feel whole and complete, worthy of love, proud and confident in who they are and who they are becoming. With a solid sense of self, they can go far and little can stop their full potential from blooming. With a solid sense of self, there of course is less fragility, which makes love and life feel less threatening. The less underlying fear and insecurity, the more ability one has to bring kindness and grace to bear in all circumstances and relationships—the crux of a moral society.

The Soul of the Matter

As we delve into this section, I'll spare you the theoretical mumbo jumbo and attempt to explain in plain language what happens when a secure attachment is formed—or not—the impact on the self, and the capacity for soulfulness. But first, a brief description of what I mean by "self" and "soul."

These terms are often used in inconsistent ways, loosely defined, and randomly thrown about. For our purposes here, the self is a psychological construct formed in the context of relationships that begins to develop with the budding awareness of being an individual, separate and distinct from others. The self encompasses conscious, unconscious and subconscious thoughts and feelings, as well as personality characteristics that make up the core of one's identity. It is essentially who one is as an individual. A solid sense of self comes through the integration of all of these parts—thoughts, feelings and the processing of life experiences. With integration, integrity of character can follow.

"Soul" as used here is an experiential construct, a quality of presence. It's an intimate relationship with one's internal life via engagement with the outer world of experiences—a visceral connection to and awareness of thoughts, feelings, sensations, insights, fantasies and reflections that create meaning and/or a deepening of experience. It is from here that purpose springs. In *Care of the Soul*, Thomas Moore refers to soulfulness as a profoundly connected, richly elaborated life.[82] And famed psychoanalyst Carl Jung, considers soulfulness to be an evolution of consciousness that brings inner peace and fulfillment. A soulful person is not at war with him or herself; they are whole and united within, a state of being complete and undivided. They are integrated.

The importance of integration has been a common theme throughout these last few chapters, important for optimal brain functioning, moral behavior, a solid sense of self and now, soulful presence. All of this grows and develops from a secure attachment—emotionally attuned relating that nurtures integration within the psyche. Yet, to one degree or another, most of us struggle to be soulfully present, fully open, engaged in and entranced by life. Something that comes naturally to a baby somehow gets lost.

We come into this world innocent, wanting nothing other than to survive by having our basic needs met. These fundamental biological needs include feeling emotionally connected, loved and cared for. Babies are pure, open-hearted beings, living in the moment with no irrational fears, only real fears related to survival. The world we're born into, however, is made up of the projected feelings, fears and thoughts of others. This is where trouble begins. The degree to which the parents' illusions thwart the ability to meet the infant/baby/child's need for simple, unadulterated love determines the health of the attachment bond.

Through our earliest experiences of human interaction, we often learn that we must feel and behave a certain way in order to receive love and affection. When love is conditional and parenting is emotionally un-attuned, it plants a deeply seated fear that being our authentic self is not enough. So, we hide behind masks to suit every person and situation. This creates a "false self," an empty inner life lived inside a protective façade, ultimately disconnected from self and thus preventing real, intimate connection with others.

With a lack of empathic attunement or "mirroring" during the growing years, we learn to disregard and lose awareness of our feeling states. Without emotional resonance from the attachment figure during the growing years, the ability to make sense and integrate our emotional experiences is compromised. When emotions are not allowed, acknowledged, or encouraged into awareness, they become a phantom part of oneself by way of suppression or repression.

Without connections with others and ourselves that bring personal meaning, life takes on a flatter, more superficial and bereft quality, breeding generalized angst from unfulfilled needs. The greater the emotional disconnection between child and parent during the developing years, the greater the disconnection within oneself, and the less capacity for full soulful presence in life.

When the inner world of thoughts and feelings is a conscious part of the self, mindful self-awareness is possible, a state where feelings can be tempered and moral choices can be made. In *Ethics for the New Millennium*, the Dalai Lama explains the importance of mindful self-awareness as understood in Tibetan culture, whereby the mind and emotions are so interrelated, they are considered one and the same:

> *"The word for mind, 'lo,' includes the ideas of consciousness, or awareness, alongside those of feeling and emotion. This reflects the understanding that emotions and thoughts cannot ultimately be separated...*
>
> *...the individual's overall state of heart and mind, or motivation, in the moment of action is, generally speaking, the key to determining its ethical content."*[83]

To be connected to one's inner experience while also being connected to, and aware of, the feeling states and perspectives of others is necessary for right action. When feeling is laced with personal meaning and self-understanding, bringing soulful reflection into the equation, a truly inside-out experience of moral and ethical direction takes place.

Nurturing Moral Intelligence

In his book, *The Moral Intelligence Of Children*, Robert Coles considers how we might best help children develop moral intelligence, which he suggests is simply knowing how to be a good person. According to him, moral intelligence involves a respect of both oneself and others, and a deep awareness of our human connectedness. Coles further elaborates that quality of character and the greatness of our humanity are expressed by how considerate, compassionate, caring, warm-hearted, unpretentious and gracefully willing to help others we are. Once again, the Golden Rule is turned to as the essential guiding principle.[84]

The not-so-good person, on the other hand, is described as being self-absorbed. If we think about it, self-absorption is almost always at the root of unethical and immoral behavior. Being swept up in an egotistic world that's all about wishes, moods, desires and demands irrespective of others is a person disconnected from empathy, compassion and any perspective outside of their own. Since there is no reflective awareness, nothing and no one exists beyond the impulse to meet self-involved needs and desires, a state usually driven by unconscious fears stemming from a fragile sense of self.

So, how is moral intelligence taught? In earlier chapters we discussed how the foundation for morality is laid through a strong attachment relationship early in life that comes from empathic attunement, and how authoritative parenting helps a child develop self-discipline, social skills and the capacity for "mindsight," the ability to put oneself in someone else's shoes. Moral intelligence is further developed and refined through meaningful relationships and life experiences. According to Coles, the most persuasive moral teaching adults do is by example. The small moments that unfold in our daily lives provide explicit and implicit lessons that shape a child's moral intelligence.[85]

Without even realizing it, children are always looking for clues in how to behave. Children are living, breathing sponges, who consciously and unconsciously perceive and mimic behaviors of those around them. Watch the mannerisms of little kids out on a soccer or baseball field, hand on hip, leg bent, weight shifted, imitating the stance of a pro with body language and attitude to match. Similarly, when it comes to moral behavior, children "absorb and take stock of what they observe, namely, us—we adults living and doing things in a certain spirit, getting on with one another in our various ways."[86] The greatest problem we face in raising moral children today is the quality of character they witness every day, on a moment-to-moment basis, not whether our culture is secular or religious. It is also our greatest solution.

Some of the most powerful messages are sent flying just under the radar of conscious awareness, yet are of weighty influence nonetheless. For instance, the mother who implores her kindergartener to share her toys, then fights with a fellow driver for the last parking spot, is sending a loud, indirect message about me first-ism. The presidential candidate, Marco Rubio—who once dropped the presidential candidates' debate to even lower levels by implying that Donald Trump's genitals were of insufficient size—sent a powerful message all over the country to any youth old enough to get the reference, especially his own. This juvenile slight issued during a nationally televised presidential debate reeked of indignity. In a desperate attempt to get the upper hand in a debate, he sold his soul. The message Rubio sent to his four children ranging in age from seven to fifteen: do anything for gain, even if it is ill-gotten gain. I wonder how they felt to witness their father's behavior. I doubt they were proud. If they were, it is cause for even more concern. Either way, this experience will undoubtedly affect them. The question is how.

As opposed to a mere intellectual understanding of right from wrong, these lessons are deeply influential because they are felt and absorbed with meaning attached via the relationship, making them indelible. This is why the "do as I say, not as I do" dictum is a hopeless one, easily shirked and readily ignored. There is no meaningful feeling derived from finger-wagging, righteous lecturing. But, when a child witnesses a parent's face light up with joy while being kind to someone, they feel the happiness. When a parent stoops to low levels for personal gain at another's expense, they feel the shame.

When it comes to examples of poor role modeling, depending on the nature of the relationship and other factors, children will either identify with the negative qualities and repeat those types of behaviors, or form a strong reaction against them, if they are old enough and reflective enough, due to some other positive influences in their life. From here they create their own personal meaning as to why they will never be like that. Either way, lessons by people who are looked up to, inherently involve meaningful emotions by virtue of the relationship and are the lessons that most profoundly reverberate.

Studies have found that when students are emotionally engaged when learning any subject, their brain is highly activated in regions all around the cortex, areas involved in cognition, memory and meaning making. This highly integrative process is what makes the lessons so resounding. When feelings are integrated with thoughts, personal meaning is created and values become woven into the soul.

This is precisely why storytelling, parables, fables and myths are so effective at conveying the moral of the story. Allegories are a creative and interpretive process where both thoughts and feelings are engaged. As Coles explains, a moral fable has magical power because of its ability to prompt a young reader's empathic response.[87] When feelings are felt and meaning is made, this creates a personalized understanding of right and wrong that provides visceral moral energy. Herein lies the moral power of the Bible and other holy texts—not as rulebooks that threaten damnation or heavenly rewards, but as parables that engage the humanity in each of us, whereby this feeling of connection inspires transcendence beyond the darker elements of human nature.

Bishop John Shelby Spong contributes some insight on this matter when he states:

"You and I are emerging people, not fallen people. Our problem is not that we are born in sin, our problem is that we don't know how to yet achieve being fully human. The function of The Christ is not to rescue the sinners, but to empower you and call you to be more deeply and fully human than you've

ever realized there was the potential within you to be. Maybe salvation needs to be conveyed in terms of enhancing your humanity, rather than rescuing you from it."[88]

Imagine if we approached raising children from this mindset— that our job was to enhance our children's humanity, to empower them to be more deeply and fully human, more connected to their thoughts and feelings, more soulful. Would this not be better than trying to create automatons following the dictates of others, empty shells with no connection to themselves and no sense of their own true north?

This would certainly require a few things from us as parents. We would have to be aware of our feelings, completely present more often than not, and have a *real* relationship with our children. By this I mean, being interested in their feelings, then wisely sharing our own in a balanced, connected and centered way. This involves having conversations with them, about them, about us, about the things that matter, rather than focusing so much on the superficial ins-and-outs, do's-and-don'ts of daily life.

If we want children to be responsive to humanity—their own and that of others—we need to share our humanity with them. Children are drawn to and intrigued by real, meaningful stories about their parents, lapping them up with wide-eyed interest. In a friendly way, we can share stories about our disappointments, fears, failures, successes, challenges, mistakes, foibles, and broken hearts. All of this lets children into our own inner world. By sharing what matters to us with them, we feed and nurture our children's souls.

Just like the rest of us, our children hunger for intimacy, physical and emotional, with the people they love. Through intimate relating as described above, children learn to make sense of the world, to understand themselves and others in relation to it, and learn to care. According to Coles, the heart of spirituality is "to look inward in search of meaning and purpose; to seek an understanding of what truly matters and for which reasons."[89] This can be nurtured in day-to-day conversations we have with our children. Too often, however, we're not even conscious to what really matters because we're caught up in a patriarchal, materialistic world that places value on the practical at the expense of the emotional and spiritual.

Contrary to what the religious right claims, secularity does not reduce the concept of morality to a question of personal choice. Rather, morality is elevated beyond dogma, beyond black-and-white rules to a spiritual level achieved by the enhancement of our humanity—being deeply rooted in personal meaning and soulful connection with self and others. Rather than traditional family values where authoritarian parenting practices figuratively and sometimes literally aim to "beat the bad" out of our children, our focus needs to be on bringing the good out of them. Family relationships that enhance our humanity through loving intimacy, warmth and acceptance, and that support the development of each individual's uniqueness are the way to do this. Now there are some family values.

7
Progressives as Protagonists in the Moral Story of America

"For what is liberty without wisdom and without virtue?
It is the greatest of all possible evils; for it is folly, vice,
madness, without tuition or restraint."

Edmund Burke, founder of modern conservatism

Along with Republicans' positioning as the party of family values, they've managed to market themselves as the party of American values as well, extending their hold on all things virtuous—family, morality and America itself. Their patriarchal, authoritarian brand of morality has become duplicitously linked with American values by the slippery use of the word "tradition." Conservatives honor tradition; therefore, traditional American values belong to Republicans. So, not only are they pro-family and pro-morals, they are pro-America. Who can argue with this? Right is obviously on their side.

Of course, embedded in their branding is the full monty assault on Democrats who they've painted as virtue less from every conceivable angle. According to their narrative, liberals are amoral, anti-family and anti-American. While this couldn't be further from the truth, Democrats have effectively succumbed to this faulty framing because they have yet to 1) deconstruct the Republican charade of moral superiority, and 2) articulate a moral narrative showing how progressive values, beliefs and positions are in fact, in alignment with America's founding principles. As we've shown in earlier chapters, progressive values jive with Jesus' message and healthy family functioning. And here we'll see how it is progressives who hew more closely to American values than modern-day conservatives.

Today's GOP seems to have lost all sense of democratic ideals, looking nothing like the party of Lincoln, lacking heart, soul, and concern for the common good. Here, we'll explore why their authoritarian values that shun wisdom and virtue in favor of dogmatism and divisiveness are detrimental to our country, contradicting the altruistic principles necessary for a democracy to thrive. And, we'll establish a moral narrative that declares progressives as protagonists in the moral story of America.

American Values: Progressive to the Core

There's nothing traditional about America—not her spirit, her charter, nor her moral foundation. And there was nothing traditional about our Founding Fathers or their vision and mission.

They were revolutionaries through and through, rebelling against the divine right of kings and ruling aristocracies. It was their principled disobedience, not subordination to authoritarian rule that inspired the very creation of our nation. Bucking tradition all the way across the Atlantic, they pursued *novus ordo seclorum*, a new order of the ages. If there is anything traditional about America, it's radical progressivism.

Our freethinking founders envisioned a new nation that embraced the will of the people, the rights of the individual, and religious freedom through a secular government. They set out to protect human rights by creating a new paradigm—a government of the people, by the people and for the people. No one had legitimate power or privilege over another—a principle in stark contrast to the hierarchical, authoritarian worldview that Republicans subscribe to today. The resolute belief in freedom, equality, and the common good—putting power and promise in the hands of all—was the driving force that birthed American democracy.

Throughout this chapter, I will turn to a governmental report, *Goals for Americans*, published in 1960, as a reference point for American values. It was commissioned by the Eisenhower administration, calling upon a non-partisan group of experts to help lay forth objectives and policies in alignment with America's founding principles. I find this report a particularly enlightening and useful reference because it was developed 1) on the cusp of our modern civil rights movement when American ideals were vigorously championed and called to the fore, and 2) before the culture wars took over our national conversation, which have made political ideology increasingly divisive and partisan agendas stubbornly entrenched. *Goals for Americans* very well could be the closest thing we have to a modern-day bastion of pure intentions for a unified government working toward common goals with coherent, well-thought-out objectives.

Before laying out any specific objectives, the report begins with the end in mind by simply stating America's overriding purpose:

"The paramount goal of the U.S. was set long ago. It is to guard the rights of the individual, to ensure his development, and to enlarge his opportunity...Our enduring aim is to build a nation and help build a world in which every human being shall be free to develop his capacities to the fullest." [90]

This goal was contrasted with the communist-oriented world in which freedom is suppressed and the individual permanently subordinated. Interestingly, we can see just how similar the goals of governing a country and governing a family in a democratic society are—to provide security, ensure development and enlarge the opportunity of its individual members. Also apparent is how alike authoritarian, traditional family values are with communist values, where freedom to be oneself is suppressed and the individual subordinated (as discussed in chapters 4 and 6). Both value systems impede the flourishing of full human potential and are thus distinctly anti-American in nature.

With the rights of the individual as an organizing principle, the role of American government is to ensure freedom (life, liberty and the pursuit of happiness), opportunity (equality), and security (common good). We'll look at each of these roles central to American government and the moral values framework necessary to achieve these goals and uphold America's core principles.

Freedom

"Life, liberty and the pursuit of happiness," likely the most referenced phrase from the U.S. Declaration of Independence, evokes the hope and grand potential that American government offers its citizens. The individual's right to live life in all its glory, to have the personal dignity that freedom allows, and to pursue happiness, as a uniquely personal quest, is the essence of American values. The tricky concept here is "pursuit of happiness," the meaning of which is questioned, debated, misunderstood and misappropriated to this day. Why did Thomas Jefferson edit out "property" from John Locke's triune of natural rights (life, liberty and property) and replace it with "the pursuit of happiness" when drafting the Declaration of Independence, and what was the meaning he intended?

It's a phrase often misconstrued and ironically used to forsake American principles. It's often cited in self-serving rationalizations that support free markets, tax cuts, limited corporate regulations, and minimal investment in the common good so that that acquiring maximum wealth, status, and material goods—the capitalist's purported path to success and happiness—can be achieved. However, there is good reason to believe that a nobler value and meaning was intended when our founding fathers put forth this organizing principle—an ethical value the Republican Party of today doesn't heed and, in fact, actively betrays.

Historians have pointed to Jefferson's embrace of Greek and Roman political philosophy that "conceived of politics as fundamentally about *relations* among those in the political community."[91] Aristotle's *Nicomachean Ethics* is often turned to for insight, a line of reasoning that associates happiness with virtue. In her article, "The Surprising Origins and Meaning of the Pursuit of Happiness,"[92] Carol V. Hamilton quotes Aristotle who wrote, "The happy man lives well and *does* well; for we have practically defined happiness as a sort of good life and good action."[93]

For Aristotle, happiness was not about having anything. It was not equivalent to wealth, honor, or pleasure but came from excellence of character, or *aretê*, the Greek word for "virtue." This virtue stems from sound character involving the right course of action, not through laws, but through the freedom to choose virtuous behavior guided by inner wisdom. It was believed that *this* produced happiness.

Hamilton further explains Jefferson's adherence to these philosophical underpinnings by way of a letter he wrote to William Short on October 13, 1819 declaring himself a disciple of Greek and Roman philosophy. She shares the content of his letter: "I consider the genuine doctrines of Epicurus as containing everything rational in moral philosophy which Greece and Rome have left us." Hamilton then provides Jefferson's summary of key points he made at the end of the letter: "Moral—Happiness the aim of life. Virtue—the foundation of happiness. Utility—the test of virtue." There's strong reason to believe that Jefferson was invoking the philosophical tradition in which happiness is bound with virtue expressed through right actions—especially civic virtues that the Greeks and Romans considered vital for the success of a community.

The Great Seal of the United States emphasizes the importance of community in our country declaring: *E pluribus Unum*, Latin for "Out of many, one." It is not, as many seem to think today, "Out of my way, while I pursue happiness." As citizens of one nation, we are united and depend on each other for success, for happiness and for a free, sound society *by way of virtue.* Benjamin Franklin astutely noted: "Only a virtuous people are capable of freedom. As nations become corrupt and vicious, they have more need of masters."[94] A self-governing democracy depends on the grace of virtue that brings country together as a community through common cause and concern—a spiritual principle akin to the Golden Rule that America's founders knew would take wisdom and grace to realize.

The Founding Fathers believed in the inherent goodness of individuals—their unlimited potential, capacity for self-governance, and commitment to the common good. They knew that liberty is a moral ideal, a spiritual concept calling for a higher conscience to rightfully consider self-serving interests within the context of community. After voyaging to America to observe and study American democracy first hand, French statesman Alexis de Tocqueville came to this very conclusion, noting: "Liberty cannot be established without morality, nor morality without faith."[95] The faith referred to here is not faith to any particular dogma, but the type of transcendent faith we established in Chapter 5 that involves overcoming ego and fear while embracing grace and forgiveness, love and compassion. Expressed in community, this takes the form of altruistic values and virtuous action.

In *Goals for Americans*, morality in the form of sound character and personal responsibility was emphasized as key to preserving the delicate balance between individual and collective interests:

"The effectiveness of a democracy—the most rewarding and most difficult form of government—rests not alone upon knowledge and judgment but upon character. Only the morally mature individual will be determined to do away with slums, end corruption and help lift the load from the poverty stricken at home and abroad. Only through moral sensitiveness can there be escape from the smugness that wealth and comfort breed. Moral sense resists avarice and self-seeking. It stimulates concern for his fellow men by which society escapes disintegration, while giving the individual maximum play for his talents, tastes, and interests."[96]

Now, *this* is the moral core of our nation—virtuous quality of character—not the nonsense we've been led to believe by the Republican branding machine that equates morality with patriarchal dominion and sexual suppression. Ignoring the personal responsibility of spiritual development and civic virtue altogether, they've managed to twist morality into something that isn't relevant to American interests or congruent with American values. A moral sense based on "concern for his fellow men," stimulates civic virtue, which is the most moral version of society that one could possibly hope for, a blending of inner spiritual life with outer life of service.

As I wrote in Chapter 5, *the highest form of moral development involves one's capacity to consider the interests of others.* "At this pinnacle of moral development, humans are capable of understanding and operating from an interest in the universal rights and needs of others, putting aside self-serving interests." This is the grand potential and the grand challenge of American democracy. Alexis de Tocqueville understood this challenge and the bold leap of faith taken by the founders who conceived of American democracy, stating: "Nothing is more fertile in the wondrous effects than the art of being free, but nothing is harder than freedom's apprenticeship."[97] It involves the spiritual values at the heart of all religion, the goal of which is to become better human beings—the ultimate personal challenge and responsibility.

As a point of contrast, let's revisit the Republicans' story of moral superiority and professed representation of American values, for it is fiction at its finest.

Their first breach of American values is their party's merger with the religious right, bringing religion head first into politics, a blatant blurring of the line between church and state, a line clearly defined by our Founding Fathers. America was not intended to be a theocracy, not even a quasi-theocracy. Ever. The religious right's attempt to turn their religious beliefs into law is a blatant assault on American democracy.

Secondly, the black-and-white moral rules set forth by Republicans' patriarchal, authoritarian worldview strip individuals of personal responsibility, which is the very essence of a free democracy. Again, as discussed in Chapter 5, embracing any kind of ideology or kowtowing to authoritarian rule actually results in the obliteration of personal choice and responsibility since there is no room to think and act in accordance with one's internal moral compass. Virtue is intertwined with freedom; we cannot have one without the other. Virtue that comes through personal responsibility is the excellence of character Aristotle refers to. Adherence to authoritarian morality *disregards the kind of personal responsibility that is necessary for a democracy to thrive.* In these ways, Republican moral values are an affront to, and antithesis of, American values. But, hang on. We're just getting started. More betrayals and contradictions are on the way.

Common Good

The Republican story of moral superiority is nothing more than a smokescreen, a distraction away from the truth—the virtue of citizens, especially civic virtues contributing to the common good, are the crux of a moral society. Their version of morality conveniently avoids this truth because it doesn't suit their interests—the common good gets in the way of "What's in it for me?"

The authoritarian attitudes prevalent in the Republican Party today suggest America is about "life, liberty and the pursuit of *my* happiness," taking the form of small government when it comes to fiscal issues—cut taxes, cut welfare programs, cut education budgets, get rid of government-funded healthcare, etc. In their worldview, minimal government involvement is the correct course when the outcome is unfettered capitalism lining pockets, feeding the greed and trampling on the common good. Yet, when it comes to private body parts and private lives (i.e., abortion, contraception, gay marriage) big government intervention is fine. Both of these positions turn American values inside out and are a contradiction to the moral foundation of America.

When a nation is built on basic respect for individual rights, its citizens are required to act with respect by way of virtue—both personal and civic—for an optimally functioning democracy. This type of virtue is derived from a soulful connection to one's sense of right and wrong via empathic connection to others. It's an internal ethical system that springs from character and becomes virtuous by way of good deed. This is the price we must pay in a free democracy—being honorable, fair, and willing to look out for others—the value of which is returned in spades by way of a fortified, cooperative and thriving society. Along with this comes the potential for fulfillment on every level for every citizen—practical, emotional, spiritual. Life, liberty and the pursuit of happiness is ours to be had—we just need a virtuous spirit to keep the dream afloat.

As discussed above, a moral core is necessary, not only to self-govern, but also to engage in civic virtues in honor of the common good. It is also imperative in choosing social responsibility and ethical behavior over the values of capitalism, which, without a keen sense of virtue, can easily slip into selfishness devoid of deeper meaning. Adam Smith, renowned philosopher and author of the classic manifesto on free-market capitalism, *An Inquiry Into the Nature and Causes of the Wealth of Nations* (1776), wrote a lesser-known treatise on human nature involving ethics and the pursuit of happiness. This work, *The Theory of Moral Sentiments*, addresses the conflict between morality and a capitalist mindset, and points out that the pursuit of money is a futile path to happiness, a particularly illuminating position for the *de facto* father of capitalism to espouse.[98]

As reported by Carol Gregoire in her article, "Before 'The Wealth of Nations', Adam Smith Penned the Ultimate Guide to a Moral Life," Smith wisely suggests that "both the individual and society benefit if we pursue our own interest through virtuous actions."[99] She distills Smith's philosophy by outlining his core beliefs, points about human nature that are remarkably similar to the points we've covered in earlier chapters.

First, Smith acknowledges that humans are both self-interested *and* designed to care about others, through empathy. It's through our ability to feel for others that makes benevolence self-gratifying; empathy counteracts selfish impulses because seeing others happy brings great pleasure. Secondly, Smith was acutely aware that we all need love, first and foremost, and it's through love, living with purpose and being appreciated and acknowledged for our contributions, that happiness is derived.

His philosophy on these matters rings true with ancient wisdom that suggests transcendence comes when embracing something greater than oneself, providing meaning and unity of spirit. Smith's insights affirm *the value of human values* above all. Coming from one of the most distinguished philosophers of modern economics, it's an opinion to carefully consider as we create government policies that involve allocation of resources and laws in support of the economic common good.

In *The American Soul: Rediscovering the Wisdom of the Founders*, Jacob Needleman reminds us: "American government was made for the purpose of protecting American society."[100] He goes on to explain how laws are designed to keep the structure of democracy in place while encouraging "the intercourse of souls in search of conscience." Laws are the "guardian of conscience,"[101] which is why we need exacting government regulations over corporations. Since corporations are entities with no soul and no conscience, American society needs to be protected from inevitable ethical breaches.

Corporations are directed by bottom line values devoid of concern for the common good, unless of course, it's the common good of shareholders. The CEOs who lead these corporations become large cogs in a soulless system, rationalizing unethical involvements, activities and practices by claiming allegiance to their purpose—to maximize profits—no matter the fallout. To hell with oceans, rainforests, clean air, untainted food, sustainable wages, economic justice, and the list goes on. For many years, the Republican Party with all the pro-corporate policies they stand for have been saying to hell with the common good—of America and the planet—and have been getting away with it virtually unchallenged.

There is a virtue deficit going on among the powers that be in corporate America, whose operating principle is: more is better, greed is good, and "what's in it for me/my company" trumps all else. A startling fact highlighting the iniquity and avarice of the corporate class was reported in *Forbes* revealing that American CEOs make an average of $11.7 million per year, *331 times* the average worker, and *774 times* minimum wage workers.[102] That means CEOs make about as much in *one day* as the average worker makes in a year, and more in one day than a minimum wage worker makes in *two* years. This article went on to explain how minimum wage workers can often not even afford to patronize the establishments they work for, such as buying cell phones from T-Mobile or dinners at Red Lobster and Olive Garden. In effect, American CEOs are "cannibalizing their own consumer base."[103] Common good? I don't think so.

Ayn Rand, whose philosophy of Objectivism has had a significant influence on libertarianism and right-wing politics, states:

"Capitalism and altruism are incompatible; they are philosophical opposites; they cannot co-exist in the same man or in the same society."[104] Well, I'm sorry to straighten out her twisted philosophy, but they have to. The essence of America involves the intricate mix of individual freedom balanced with the common good. It is Rand's brand of capitalism that is incompatible with American values, values that are fundamentally altruistic in nature. As for coexistence, there is no such thing as peaceful, functional coexistence in a society without altruism. Our founders knew this, which accounts for the emphasis on the common good and why spiritual enlightenment was considered essential to a functioning democracy. Based on our country's principles, it's Rand's type of capitalism that should not exist in American society.

Altruism and the capacity to feel empathy is hardwired into our brain circuitry; it's a human instinct crucial for bonding and survival. Altruism is simply the behavioral expression of empathy. Rand's break in logic occurs with her extremist view that being altruistic is being self-sacrificing. She states:

"The irreducible primary of altruism, the basic absolute, is self-sacrifice—*which means; self-immolation, self-abnegation, self-denial, self-destruction*—which means: the self *as a standard of evil, the* selfless *as a standard of the good."*[105]

There are many things wrong with Rand's reasoning. First, she fails to see that lending a hand, offering assistance, contributing to others, and other acts of giving are not *ipso facto* destructive acts of self-sacrifice. For human beings with their soul intact, there is pleasure in these exchanges, as Adam Smith, the granddad of capitalism, reminds us. We feel good when we see others feel good, so we benefit when others benefit. Rand's Objectivism is so rational that she negates human emotion entirely and approaches her theories on capitalism like a computer with binary, black-and-white concepts, completely lacking human elements—emotions or feelings, heart or soul. Whether she likes it or not, capitalism is an economic system embedded in a larger system known as society which is made up of living, breathing, feeling human beings—a social system the American government is designed to protect.

Second, no one is asking anyone to self-immolate, or as Rand says elsewhere, to be "a sacrificial animal to be immolated for the benefit of the group..."[106] This rhetoric is so far over the top that it's a wonder anyone has ever taken her seriously. I hardly think expecting CEOs to scale back their $11 million a year salaries so their employees can be rightly compensated is self-immolation. Expecting corporations to not rape the environment in pursuit of profit is not self-abnegation. Refraining from cheating the middle class with off-shore tax shelters is not self-denial. Resisting the urge to outsource U.S.-based businesses overseas is not an undue sacrifice, any more than refraining from poisoning our air, food and water is self-destruction, and on and on. These regulations are merely attempts to infuse capitalism with ethical principles in order to reign in exploitation and protect the greater interest. It's true that profits would likely be affected by these actions, but that is a far cry from immolating, denying and destroying corporations by these common good practices. For all her steely Objectivism, our Ayn is a touch melodramatic.

As America has become more and more enamored with material wealth, sucked deep into capitalism as an organizing principle impacting life's every purpose, the notion of individualism that our founders intended has degenerated from a spiritual ideal into self-indulgence and self-righteous indignation. In *The American Soul*, Needleman explains individualism as an Enlightenment ideal that was derived from ancient wisdom. He reminds us that American individualism was conceived as a deeply authentic engagement with "the force of I," the freedom to be self-directed by a transcendent inner knowing and soulful connection with one's purpose.

> *"Independence is understood as the discovery of one's own authentic self...equality is understood as every human being's right to seek the truth and be allowed to give his or her light to the common welfare"* [107]

According to Needleman, it's this type of individualism that forms the basis of the American ideal, and the *reason* that Jefferson and the Enlightenment philosophers used as their guiding principle.

> *"Reason was the realm of human freedom, the realm in which, from the interior of the self, a man or woman could open to the need both to function well in the earthly life we are given and at the same time to receive life and vision from a realm of reality beyond what the ordinary senses and passions recognized."* [108]

If we could bring individualism as soulful wisdom into capitalism we would not find egregious greed, but capitalism with a conscience, something that works for each and every individual as well as the common good. It's individualism that results in care about individuals where the "divine knowing" involves empathy and compassion and the Golden Rule takes primacy over the "the hell with you" rule. As Martin Luther King Jr. noted in his *Conquering Self-Centeredness* speech in 1957:

> *"An Individual has not started living fully until they can rise above the narrow confines of individualistic concerns to the broader concerns of humanity. Every person must decide at some point, whether they will walk in the light of creative altruism or in the darkness of destructive selfishness. This is the judgment: Life's most persistent and urgent question is: 'What are you doing for others?'"* [109]

Equality

The notion that all men are created equal and America are nearly synonymous—you hear one, and think of the other. Liberty and its counterpart, equal opportunity, provide the hope that defines America and has inspired her many immigrants seeking a better, just life where ingenuity and hard work could be rewarded, no matter your status, race, religion or creed. The U.S. government has been designed to protect these rights, but translating the ideal of equality into reality has been one of America's greatest challenges. The reasons for this are complex, involving the ever-present shadow side of human nature, national history, social conditioning, personal ancestry and personal demons that create divisiveness and enmity rather than unity and harmony. Embracing equality requires the human race to overcome the Achilles heel embedded in our very makeup—the tendency to react defensively in fear (of differences, scarcity, disempowerment, the unknown, etc.) rather than respond with an open, inclusive, caring heart. Even though there have been setbacks along the way, America as a whole continues to persevere on this uphill climb toward equality.

At a crucial time in history, *Goals for Americans* reaffirmed the need to continue working toward greater equality, pronouncing in 1960 before the civil rights movement:

> *"Vestiges of religious prejudice, handicaps to women, and, most important, discrimination on the basis of race must be recognized as morally wrong, economically wasteful, and in many respects dangerous. In this decade we must sharply lower these last stubborn barriers...Respect for the individual means respect for every individual...One role of government is to stimulate changes of attitude."*[110]

In that decade and the decades to follow, great strides have been made in the areas of race, gender and now, sexual orientation. Our history is full of civil rights causes gradually tipping the scales toward a more equal and just society through progressive politics and activism against forces that attempt to maintain the social, economic and political status quo of white male power. The pushback against equality inevitably comes from the Republicans among us, with their authoritarian worldview, a value system involving personality characteristics that readily perceives those who are different as a threat, who derive a feeling of security by having the hierarchical structure of white male dominance kept in place, and who use anger to cope with their fear of differences—disregarding, suppressing or attacking those who embody the other.

Prejudices are both explicitly and implicitly expressed through conventional attitudes that disfavor anyone who is not a white male in familiar assumptions, such as: a black boy in a hoodie is a dangerous threat, a woman is not as capable on the job as a man, an illegal alien is a lazy freeloader. Those who are discriminated against feel these slights clearly as day, creating a sense of injustice rightly leading to societal unrest. Lately, a recent spate of unjust police brutality toward young black men and racial inequality in the criminal justice system is creating societal outrage fueling a "Black Lives Matter" movement, which will hopefully create a tipping point to right this wrong.

Whenever it becomes united we stand, divided we fall into the haves and have nots, the blacks and whites, the men and women, liberals and conservatives, the immigrants and natural born citizens, our democracy is weakened. Internal strife, essentially a micro-level civil war against our very own neighbors, is counter to our goals. We're not on different teams. We're fellow Americans who share common ground, common purpose, and a responsibility for the common good.

With prejudices so prevalent, the question becomes: Is America really committed to human equality? If so, is it all of us, or just the progressives among us? Indeed, for many conservatives these principles seem to be empty platitudes at best, or a cause to be resisted, at worst. One of the best examples of empty platitudes with confounding effect comes from former Republican Speaker of the House Newt Gingrich. The American Heritage project quotes Gingrich who states:

> *"With the declaration, America set itself apart, an exception from the ways of the other nations of the world, and embarked on a radically new course in history, in pursuit of neither wealth, nor power, nor racial or ethnic purity, but an idea: God-given liberty for all."*[111]

Ironically, this comes from a man who was responsible for the infamous welfare reform in the 1990's that was widely criticized for being motivated by racism and misogyny. It was sold to the public with rhetoric based on stereotypes portraying those in need, typically African-American single mothers, as "welfare queens" having every type of character deficiency imaginable. While these policies succeeded in decreasing government welfare, they did nothing to solve the real problem—helping the underprivileged escape from poverty with job opportunities that offered enough pay for financial security and independence. Under such circumstances, there is no possible way to become equal, self-supporting contributors to society. The authoritarian, "pull yourself up by your bootstraps" brand of moralizing does not help the less fortunate get on their feet, nor does pulling the rug out from underneath those boots, but it does do a good job shifting blame and shirking responsibility for the common good.

What was once considered the formula for success—get an education, get a job, get married before having children—is a bogus template that no longer allows people to escape poverty. While conservatives like to blame poverty on lack of traditional family structure, research reported in a brief released by *Council of Contemporary Families* shows that poverty is not due to family structure, but to growing inequality and income insecurity. In 1965, a one-worker family of three with a minimum wage job working 40 hours a week could keep their family just above the poverty line. In 2012, a family of three, one member working 40 hours a week at minimum wage puts them below the poverty line at about 78%, and if two parents work, the cost of childcare keeps them below the line.[112] There is no way out.

When full-time employment results in poverty, there is something seriously wrong with our economic system. Workers we depend on daily—firefighters, teachers, police—cannot financially sustain themselves in many of the communities they serve. Somebody has to do those jobs, and those somebodies have a right to live a life that provides for their needs. These are not lazy people wanting to be the so-called "takers from the makers." These are people trapped in a system that does not allow for independent survival based on effort, never mind progress. As family historian Stephanie Coontz recently reported, there has been a "broadly based increase in income insecurity that is concentrated neither among low-skill workers, nor single-parent families"[113] Gross income inequality is spreading dramatically.

Today obscene amounts of wealth belong in the hands of a few, sucking the middle class dry. To quote 2016 Democratic presidential candidate Bernie Sanders' oft-repeated fact "the top one-tenth of one percent owns almost as much wealth as the bottom 90 percent." As Sanders asserted, "There is something profoundly wrong when *one family* owns more wealth than the bottom *130 million* Americans."[114] Indeed. Capitalism has gone right off the moral rails along with the Republican Party. The system is rigged to funnel even more wealth to the wealthiest, as Sanders often reminded us. This type of inequality is unequivocally against everything America stands for, yet has become institutionalized by politicians through deregulation that does nothing but assist corporations and those who run them get wealthier with offshore tax havens, tax loopholes, overseas manufacturing, the exportation of jobs, etc., at the expense of the common good.

And while the wealthy get wealthier, the middle class is disappearing altogether as two-earner families run ragged, getting nowhere fast. Forget about getting ahead, many can't even get by because our economic system does not support the common needs of the common person. Things that should be a given in a first world nation like America such as health care, college education, affordable housing, and enough income to invest for retirement funds are not. One startling statistic states that 60% of yearly bankruptcies in the U.S. are due to medical expenses.[115] If an average person cannot get the medical intervention that they or their loved ones need without foreclosing on their home and going bankrupt, we have a broken system. If an average family needs to take a second mortgage out on their home to send their children to college, we have a broken system. If a college student has to amass tens of thousands of dollars in debt in order to graduate, and that puts them in a hole so deep it takes on average 21 years to pay off, we have a broken system.

Unfortunately, these scenarios are not hypotheticals; they are real challenges faced every day. There's a tremendous red flag flapping so bright and so large we can no longer ignore the fact we have strayed far away from the principle of equality. The problem isn't inequality of income; that's expected in a capitalist society. It's the *gross* inequality of resources and funds, the result of a broken system that does not do what it is supposed to do—provide equal opportunity for the betterment of all.

American democracy is not supposed to function like a "Survival of the Richest" reality TV show where winner takes all and the poor and middle class are voted off the island, out of the running for a financially secure life. Even though we give lip service to equality and believe our country is one of meritocracy, today only the privileged class has a toehold that allows any movement up the so-called ladder of success, while the rest get swallowed up in debt. *The Meritocracy Myth* (2004), challenges the fabled American notion that hard work paves the way to success and shows how societal inequalities play a larger role in determining who gets ahead today.[116] The authors make a strong case that the amount of income, wealth and success one has is based on what one owns, not how hard one works. With America gradually turning into an oligarchy, our democracy is eroding right before our eyes. As the late Supreme Court Justice, Louis Brandeis once admonished, "We can either have democracy in this country or we can have great wealth concentrated in the hands of a few, but we can't have both."[117]

Inequality of all types is an assault to our foundational principles, weakening our democracy in every way imaginable. In *Goals for Americans*, the problem of inequality was succinctly stated:

"Needless barriers inevitably create and constantly multiply bitterness against a system which not only tolerates but ensures frustration. Whatever is done to foment resentment lays the

axe at the root of the system of government to which we are committed."[118]

It's been speculated that the rise of the anti-establishment demagogue Donald Trump was a result of this very frustration. People knew that the system was not working for them, and rightly didn't trust politicians to fix it, so they turned to Trump. He became the leading contender among disaffected working class voters because he was a figure through whom they could channel their frustration and anger. It didn't matter that he was making a mockery of our great democracy and didn't have anywhere near the kind of wisdom or virtue one would expect from a president. This unfathomable turn of events showed just how vulnerable to breakdown our democracy can be. The risk of electing a president—the ultimate representative of the United States—who does not represent the American values our founders envisioned in any way, shape, or form has never been more clear.

A *New York Times* article points out how the handiwork of the Republican Party has created the "needless barriers fomenting resentment" above. It explains:

"...by years of systematically and effectively preventing passage of legislation that might have ameliorated the tough economic state of Mr. Trump's core voters. Mr. Trump's biggest supporters are disproportionately white, middle-aged, working-class men without college educations, a group whose fortunes have flagged as globalization and new technology have rendered millions of jobs obsolete and cut into the wages of many more. While the trade agreements that Mr. Trump bashes have

played a role, the mistake was not having entered into them,
but having failed to sufficiently help affected workers adjust to
the new dynamics."[119]

In effect, the Republican Party has been operating as destruc-
tionists, laying "the axe at the root of the system of government,"
patently not supporting America and her values.

And it gets even worse. Racism, xenophobia and misogyny are
commanding the Republican stage as well. Prejudicial attitudes
are used to rally voters while Trump incites aggression among
his supporters toward whatever flavor-of-the-day "out group" is to
blame for all that is wrong in America. The fact that both Trump
and the equally racist, xenophobic, misogynistic and distasteful
Ted Cruz, more of a covert operator, were once the dual leading
contenders in the Republican Party, underscores the degree to
which authoritarianism has unreservedly taken over the party,
while establishment conservatives were horrified. Not, if truth be
told, by the attitudes displayed, but by the fact their dirty little
secret was out in the open. Their dog-whistle prejudices once
only expressed in coded language and behind closed doors were
now unabashedly paraded to great applause among way too many
Americans, mostly the less educated, whose resentment over our
broken government appears to have taken the greatest toll.

Though mainstream Republicans claimed innocence and
distanced themselves from Trump, the problem was not Trump.
He did not cause the septic mess witnessed today; he was merely
the hot compress making contact with a festering boil, bringing
it all to a head. Divisiveness, fear and bigotry have been infect-
ing our government in a passive-aggressive manner for decades,

most recently manifested in Congressional gridlock and dirty politics (such as flat-out refusing to consider President Obama's Supreme Court nomination), race-wars, religious wars, and fear-mongering—all everyday fare in our political theater.

In *Goals for Americans*, equality among citizens was addressed as a pressing moral issue: "It is beyond question that feelings and acts of prejudice are corrosive of the moral integrity of our people."[120] In light of this proclamation and based on what we are witnessing in the Republican Party, we can deduce that Republican values are caustic to the moral integrity of our country. It goes on to say, "A new moral outlook is more important than new legislation."[121] Throwing every immigrant out on their ear or banning all Muslims from entering our country, as both Trump and Cruz promised to do if elected, are prime examples.

The popularity of this borderline fascist, authoritarian brand of righteous disregard and contemptuous bullying has been a profound wake-up call, alerting us to just how far our government, particularly the Republican Party, has strayed from the principles of a liberal democracy. I imagine our Founding Fathers are spinning in their graves to the point of nausea, witnessing the lunacy unfold that has no resemblance to the America they set out to create, one reliant upon wisdom and virtue as her guiding force. We have devolved into what Edmund Burke, the great political philosopher and founder of modern conservatism had warned against—liberty without wisdom and virtue is the greatest of all possible evils. With liberty and justice for folly, vice, and madness is not what our founders had in mind.

Despite painting themselves with red, white and blue hues, the Republican claim of embracing traditional American values is an offensive pretense, and it's time to call them out on it. Republicans today are, in fact, in absolute betrayal of America—her altruistic principles, her grace, and her glory—and are sliding headfirst into a moral sinkhole with no return. Let's not let America get sucked down with them.

Reclaiming the Soul of America: Moving Forward with Moral Conviction

The birth of this country was an audacious, profound and optimistic effort to forge a government based on moral and spiritual values involving freedom, equality and the common good, something never before realized. These American values have been trampled on and disregarded by modern-day Republicans who have expertly turned their very transgressions back on Democrats, deriding them for altruistic concerns, as if they weren't real American values. While distorting facts and obscuring truth, Republicans have convincingly, yet undeservedly, asserted the moral high ground and have blamed Deomcrats for all that is wrong in our country. No more.

It's apparent the Republican Party has lost all moral *gravitas*, and Democrats no longer have to tiptoe around the Republican frame of moral superiority. Democrats no longer have to move center to appeal to "values voters," nor should they. Democrats no longer have to kowtow to people whose purse strings are in politics, nor should they—ever. With a strong, stirring moral narrative grounded in American values, Democrats can tap into the heart and soul of the American people. A populist uprising can change the moral turpitude that has become our government, filling our current system's moral abyss with the moral conviction of a progressive movement.

Now is the time for progressives to pick up the ball and run with the very audacity, profundity and optimism that drove our founders. It's time to boldly set course to save America's grace, to overcome authoritarianism with altruism backed by a moral outrage rightly possessed in face of the farce that is the Republican Party.

Worthy of our attention here is the quote by Teddy Roosevelt from Chapter 1: "Remember: The most perfect machinery of government will not keep us as a nation from destruction if there is not within us a soul."[122] With little to no soulful reflection in the Republican Party today, this danger is imminent. We see arrogant moral righteousness turn into shameful, jaw-dropping hypocrisy time and again. We see reactionary partisanship that exudes the emotional maturity of a toddler, heels dug in, refusing to eat their broccoli. We see cruel and calculating one-upmanship among presidential candidates acting like members of a mob, vying for alpha status. And we see leadership with a pathetic lack of acuity equal to that of the proverbial blind man—in this instance blind to ethics, to virtue and to the value of inner wisdom. No more.

The political division our nation is entrenched in goes right down to the core of who we are as a people, as a culture, and as a nation. It's a split between altruism and authoritarianism, between soulfulness and self-righteousness, between care and cynicism. It is, frankly, a good vs. evil battle for virtue, for American principles and national integrity. If we lose sight of these higher elements of human nature, we will inevitably devolve as a society and as a government, and lose the hope that is America.

The Dalai Lama addressed this very point with his signature wisdom: "Through lack of basic human feeling, religion, politics, economics and so on can be rendered dirty. Instead of serving humanity, they become agents of its destruction."[123] We've been witnessing the unabashed dirtying of principles for far too long, and if this course is not turned around, we may face the very destruction to which the Dalai Lama refers. Looking back at our earlier chapters, we discussed the GOP's dirtying of religious principles and the true message of Jesus, the dirtying of capitalistic principles and the substance of Adam Smith, and in this chapter, the GOP's dirtying of democratic principles and the aspiration of our founders. Even though proclaiming allegiance to these ideals, Republicans have bastardized them all, stripping them of feeling and of soul, changing the intent entirely.

Authoritarians' signature characteristic is an ignoble, prideful stance in lack of basic human feeling. While some may think this is important for leadership, it's quite the contrary. Serving humanity requires a feeling for humanity, something today's Republicans seem to have forgotten. Instead, they seem hell-bent on pursuing their soulless crusade to further empower the powerful and enrich the rich while demoralizing the demoralized. Our challenge is to bring feeling back into politics while revealing the contemptuous narrative about human feeling for what it is—a desperate attempt to undermine altruism for the sake of selfish concerns.

Republicans have been experts at turning this very deficiency (lack of soulful feeling) back on Democrats, painting progressives as soft, bleeding-heart liberals with broad, cynical strokes designed to emasculate any effort toward goodwill. Since 9/11, authoritarianism in politics seems to have gotten the upper hand and anything that doesn't reek of toughness is derided as weak and un-American.

During the 2012 presidential campaign, right-wing politicians and pundits took to using "Kumbaya" as sneering shorthand toward anyone showing a shred of compassion, or attempting to seek peaceful agreement and compromise. Ironically, "Kumbaya," is a *traditional American* folk song inspiring togetherness by appealing to God to help those in need. It's a deeply spiritual song that the callous Right mocks as un-American with their flippant use of the reference. How ironic. The pious party of traditional American values points to a spiritual song rooted in American culture as being un-American. God help us, indeed.

How distorted have we become? As commentary on *NPR* pointed out "Rather than Kumbaya representing strength and power in togetherness and harmony as it once did, the word has come to reflect weakness and wimpiness....Kumbaya" hasn't changed, but America has."[124] Once again, we can see how "the hell with you" rule, not the Golden Rule, best sums up Republican values. *This* is the great shame, not altruism.

It's time to take the soul castrating power away from Republicans and reinstate, reinforce and reinvigorate the soul of America. We can't let their cynical bullying detract from the truth. Virtuous goodwill *is* the best of America. It is the Republicans who are disgracefully out of sync with American values. In fact, more Americans than not are altruistic at heart.

According to the American Values Survey conducted by the Public Religion Research Institute (2015) nearly two-thirds (65%) of Americans believe that "one of the big problems in this country is that we don't give everyone an equal chance in life," and more than three-quarters (76%) of Americans support raising the minimum wage from $7.25 to $10.10 per hour.[125] This means that at least this many Americans hold altruistic values, a moral worldview that has yet to be presented as the correct course for government aims across various issues. It's up to Democrats to articulate and represent these moral views. It's up to Democrats to take a stand for democracy and the principles of freedom, equality, and the common good. It's up to Democrats to promote a moral narrative that inspires attitudes and policies grounded in altruism—the soul of America depends on it.

As Thomas Jefferson famously said: "The care of human life and happiness, and not their destruction, is the first and only object of good government."[126] It's important to clarify that being altruistic means just this, not what Republicans fear it means—encouraging dependency on the government, like a baby on a mother's teat. That is not good for anyone, including the reliant if they are capable. An altruistic intent does whatever can be done to provide the support, resources and opportunities needed to help every citizen develop solid independence and maximize their life potential. As a society and as a culture, we are strengthened when optimum potential is realized, no matter who or what that life potential is.

One obvious example would be ensuring access to education in all areas relevant to solid independent functioning. This includes academic or vocational schools, science-based family life and parenting education, and education in civics and finances. It's shocking how little most Americans know about the importance of compassionate childrearing (the foundation of creating a sound society), our political process, managing money, investments and the wise or unwise use of credit. While banks and corporations profit off consumerism-gone-mad and credit cards maxed to the hilt with never-ending interest payments, the rest of us don't.

In *Goals for Americans*, the need to invest in education was addressed, declaring: "This is at once an investment in the individual, in the democratic process, in the growth of the economy and in the stature of the United States."[127] An educated citizenship ultimately benefits society as a whole. The only people who benefit from an uneducated society are those in power who want to remain in power.

Nor does being altruistic mean being soft on terrorists or craven in the face of any national threats. While the Republicans promise, with grandiose flair, to rid the world of evildoers with their War on Terrorism, this doesn't mean their approach is better, stronger or even sensible. The conversation here needs to turn to the discernment between strength and aggression, between strategy and brute force, and between patriotism and nationalism. As laid out in *Goals for Americans*, published in the midst of Cold War tensions:

> "Our position before the world should be neither defensive nor belligerent...We should seek to mitigate tensions, and search for acceptable areas of accommodation with opponents."[128]

Accordingly, caution and non-aggression should always be the baseline *modus operandi*, with the judicious use of force considered only when necessary—a well-conceived strategy that is precise, deliberate and diplomatically sophisticated. If innocent civilians can be spared and some modicum of goodwill can be communicated, we can further the goal of reining in, rather than inflaming, anti-American sentiment. It takes brains, not bombs, to address the roots of terrorism. The commonly heard phrase, "You can't bomb beliefs" is an undeniable truth; bombs only solidify what they are trying to destroy—extremist beliefs.

Altruism doesn't mean rolling over passively, but it echoes the moral elegance of Theodore Roosevelt's dictum: "Speak softly and carry a big stick." Being ready and willing to use force when necessary is much different than today's GOP approach—beating war drums and thumping chests in a histrionic display of nationalism that is provocative, threatening and simply unwise. Upping the ante is the last thing we need to do with terrorists because they have no upper limits. Also, this feeds into their story of American imperialism and aggression, which only validates terrorist propaganda.

In order to begin shifting the moral tenor of our government and making these big, bold changes, the place to start is with campaign finance reform. Money and politics are a corrosive mix, like moisture on steel. In order to bring our government back to where it belongs, in the hands of the people, we need to stop private funding of campaigns and lobbyists. This is the only way to give common people power, and bring humanistic values back into politics—by reining in capitalistic values that have corrupted our democracy and taken over the soul of our country.

We have a unique challenge before us. Overcoming authoritarianism with altruism is difficult by virtue of the very qualities inherent in those with these opposing worldviews. Authoritarians tend to be fearful and angry, driven to assert power whenever, wherever, and in whatever way they can in order to obtain some feeling of safety and control. They make it their mission to be on the attack and to undermine opposition groups. They're fighters who are only comfortable when fighting. Altruists, on the other hand, don't naturally have this edge. They're optimistic and less cynical. They empathize. They contemplate. They parse. They logically lay out arguments. This is not what we need at this juncture. It's time to put aside equanimity. It's time to find that edge, the outraged edge, and employ it.

It is the angry who are energized, who make noise and who make themselves heard. We need to tap into the anger of injustice, which is a very different type of anger than the anger that authoritarians wield, which springs from hate. As Marianne Williamson eloquently implored, it's time to embody moral outrage with "a reawakening of the original revolutionary spirit"[129] that our founders embraced, revolutionaries with a purpose propelled by moral conviction. She later stated:

> "One of the reasons those who hate have become so loud is because those of us who love have loved too quietly. Conviction is a force multiplier. Those who hate have displayed more conviction than do those of us who love. Love must expand beyond the confines of personal relationships to become a collective force for social and political change. Gandhi said it, Martin Luther King Jr. said it, and boy does it ring true now."[130]

Our only hope is for progressives to dig down deep to find the conviction to fight for what's right. To fight for and from love with as much vigor as those who fight for and from hate. To fight the good fight because not to wouldn't be right. Republicans have taken great joy in ridiculing Democrats for having no moral conviction, only charts and data. That story is over.

It's time to remind our nation that progressives are the protagonists in the moral story of America—a point made so passionately and so clearly, it's a mic drop. As former President Calvin Coolidge once said, "Little progress can be made by merely attempting to repress what is evil. Our great hope lies in developing what is good."[131] It's up to progressives to fight the good fight, to continue to feel the burn that Bernie Sanders sparked, no matter who is in, or out, of the White House. Let's do this. For us. For our children. For the future of America.

8
A New Solution:
From Culture War to
Cultural Evolution

"...if we are to survive today, our moral and
spiritual "lag" must be eliminated. Enlarged material
powers spell enlarged peril if there is not
proportionate growth of the soul."

Martin Luther King, Jr.

F or decades, the religious right has been waging a culture war
in attempt to save America from the devil's embrace. While
our society has lost its moral footing and our coarse culture leaves
much to be desired, the actual problem, causes and solutions laid
forth by the so-called culture warriors are woefully off the mark.
They've not only been climbing up the wrong tree, they've been
lost in a forest without a compass. Lacking true north, no amount

of direction will help the sorry state our culture is in. It's time to find the right direction.

These misguided moralists have been warring against what they believe are cultural evils—i.e., fact-based sex education and the teaching of evolution in schools, marriage equality, the provision of birth control in health insurance plans, which public restrooms transsexuals may use, and for the "religious freedom" to discriminate against homosexuals in whatever manner they choose, etc. Their ill-conceived narrative of the moral problems and solutions facing our country has been swallowed hook, line and sinker, and has been injected into our national conversation so thoroughly that we've lost all perspective of the real ethical and moral troubles at hand. Contrary to their view, America is not being destroyed by homosexuals, liberals or any aspect of a secular society. The fundamental problem we face as a culture is this: *Capitalistic values have overtaken humanistic values, hollowing out the soul of our society.*

Entrenched in bottom line concerns, mindless materialism, and the all-consuming need to one-up the next, we've lost sight of what really matters. Humanistic values and integrity of character have fallen by the wayside on the road to success. Conducting oneself with class—complimenting a competitor, extending a hand to someone in need, showing modesty in the face of good fortune (be it wealth, beauty, status or success) and defining a life well-lived by the amount of love and good grace given and received—is no longer *de rigueur* for a dignified life. In fact, it seems that a dignified life is not even an aspiration to strive for.

Our values are so upside down that upstanding character does not rise to the top in our society, the dregs do. Donald Trump and the Kardashian clan epitomize all that is wrong in America—the lack of taste, grace and moral sensibility—yet we celebrate them as if they embody all that is honorable. Currently, Trump is the presumptive Republican nominee for President of the United States, a shell of a person who lacks thoughtful reflection or leadership capacity beyond trampling over others on his way to the top. And the Kardashians have been anointed celebrity status with multi-million-dollar endorsement and media deals by virtue of their boorish lifestyle that's obsessively followed and worshipped by the masses. One magazine went so far as to refer to them as "America's Royal Family"—an indictment of a culture that has lost all sense of true pride and dignity. The only bowing before the Kardashians that I would do involves picking my jaw up off the ground in disbelief over their utter ignorance and lack of respectability.

That which they and Trump personify, and which we as a culture seem to esteem, is narcissistic self-involvement of the shallowest sort. *This* is the moral abyss in which our culture has landed—a soulless disconnection from ourselves, others, and that which gives life meaning. It's truly astounding that Trump's juvenile insults and the Kardashians' silicone-boosted body parts garner more interest and media attention than the devastating crises around the world. Incessant wars in the Middle East where innocent civilians are bombed daily, Syrian refugees risking their lives in the diminishing hope of life elsewhere, and the plight of millions around the world suffering from disease and hunger don't grab our attention like the crass and puerile. How can this be?

As a culture and as people we've become unmoored from our souls, oblivious to that which makes us human. In our fast-paced, capitalistic society we've had our eye on the prize of the almighty dollar at the expense of living meaningful, deeply felt, and connected lives—lives where the care and concern of others brings more fulfillment than purchasing power, where truly engaging with each other in the here and now, eye to eye, is more important than any smartphone distraction, where we support our children's development by modeling grace and civility not pitiable get-ahead attitudes, and where it's more important to wear our humanity on our sleeve than name-brand logos.

Through generations of programming telling us to focus on outer rewards rather than our inner world of feeling and meaning, telling us that our value is derived from what we make and own rather than who we are, we've been taught to operate without being grounded in our hearts, in our minds, in our souls. This type of depersonalization and dehumanization has had a tragic effect on our culture.

In his book, *Ethics for the New Millennium*, the Dalai Lama contends that ethical problems, both personal and cultural, are due to neglect of our inner dimension. He goes on to explain that this neglect is a spiritual crisis of the most dire sort, and nothing short of a spiritual revolution—not a political revolution, economic revolution or technological revolution—will significantly alleviate the problems we face.[132] In his view, the ultimate objective of this spiritual revolution is "a radical reorientation away from our habitual preoccupation with the self."[133]

He then makes a clear distinction between religion and spirituality, a crucial point in our increasingly pluralistic world where common ground, not differences, need to be emphasized for harmony to be achieved. According to the Dalai Lama, religion, which is concerned with dogmatic beliefs, adherence to ritual, prayer to one's God and faith in salvation, isn't necessary to be ethical. Rather, he sees spirituality as the essence of ethical behavior, encompassing any and all, or no religion. One thing it does involve are "those qualities of the human spirit—such as love and compassion, patience, tolerance, forgiveness, contentment, a sense of responsibility, a sense of harmony—which bring happiness to both self and others..."[134]

No, the problem we need to be warring against is not the lack of religious rule as the culture warriors suppose, but the emotionally and spiritually impoverished culture in which we live. As Martin Luther King, Jr. warned in his 1964 Nobel Peace Prize address, "The Quest for Peace and Justice":

"Our problem today is that we have allowed the internal to become lost in the external. We have allowed the means by which we live to outdistance the ends for which we live. So much of modern life can be summarized in that arresting dictum of the poet Thoreau: 'Improved means to an unimproved end.' This is the serious predicament, the deep and haunting problem confronting modern man...If we are to survive today, our moral and spiritual 'lag' must be eliminated. Enlarged material powers spell enlarged peril if there is not proportionate growth of the soul. When the 'without' of man's nature subjugates the within,' dark storm clouds begin to form in the world."[135]

Dark storm clouds are here. Our material powers have dwarfed the growth of the soul many times over, skewing our values with perverted notions of what really matters.

As a society, we lack a connection to something greater than capitalistic standards of well-being. Spiritual impoverishment coupled with capitalism creates limitless greed and hunger. It is like a tapeworm in the soul. No matter how many things we acquire, or how much power or wealth we achieve, it will never be enough. Corporate America takes advantage of this insatiable hunger, convincing us through advertising that consumerism will soothe our problems. If we buy, we will then be more popular, youthful, sexy, attractive, enviable, successful, happy, and the list goes on. It's the hungry soul that drives the culture of consumption. Capitalism thrives on it; humanity suffers from it, sending us on a futile chase for peace and contentment that can never be found in the material world.

How can we begin to turn this around?

One of the first steps toward a cultural evolution is the act of becoming aware of the depraved forces in our culture that have molded our values and defined our identities, hollowing out our souls. By depraved, I'm not referring to the traditional notions of sin. I'm talking about the crude, shallow and narcissistic climate in which we live and embody. The offense is not against God, but against our human spirit. We live contrary to our need for greater meaning and soulful authenticity, lapping up the artificial and superficial that leaves us emotionally hungry and spiritually empty. To cite a few examples:

- We're obsessed with phony people and scripted lives on "reality" TV, living vicariously through the indiscreet antics of others.
- We consume photo-shopped media, whereby unreal images become the impossible ideals we hopelessly seek.
- We admire faces stripped of any trace of age, unique character or personal story, preferring a fake, plastic look to natural beauty.
- We seek to "love" our bodies by surgically vacuuming out fat and implanting silicone to the point of cartoonish distortion.
- Sexuality is removed from genuine beauty of person, spirit and intimacy. Objectification is considered sexy and addictive use of porn has become a sad and desperate attempt to connect with sexual feelings.
- We focus on our kids doing, doing, doing rather than simply being. We care more about them being the best at anything and everything, than how they emotionally function in the world, whether they're stressed out or well-adjusted, kind people.
- We watch rant and slant "news" shows filled with irrational, contemptuous sparring, with little fact or in-depth analysis that could enlighten rather than enrage.
- We care more about having the "right" labels than living within our means, or helping people in need.
- We're constantly exposed to gratuitous violence in the media, spawning a numbing effect and disconnection from human suffering.

Rather than a culture war, per se, I propose a cultural *evolution*—a movement toward greater consciousness that involves a reconnection with the inner dimension where our deeper human needs dwell. In order to enhance our society and culture, we need to enhance our humanity. To do this we need more empathy. More compassion. More meaning. More soul. And the place to begin is in the family.

There is a fundamental truth to the adage "humanity passes by way of the family;" the family is the fertile field where children develop. How grounded they become and how well they are shaped is determined by the emotional quality of family relationships. It is also this very same emotional quality that determines the health of marriages and overall function of the family. For better or for worse, families are human systems driven by emotional needs and dynamics. To ignore this fact is to remain ignorant of the inner workings of family life that can make or break us as individuals and as a culture.

Indeed, it's the conventional mores disregarding our emotional needs that have landed us in the mess we're in. Authoritarian, traditional family values squelch the soul while capitalistic values disregard the soul. Both disconnect us from our human essence, our inner emotional world where empathy is born, love grows, meaning is made, life is enriched, and self-awareness takes form. It's from here, and only from here, that the greatest elements of our humanity can emerge. It is from here, and only from here, that a cultural evolution is possible.

Rather than seeing the loss of traditional family values as a sign of Armageddon, we can view ourselves as being in the midst of an evolutionary step forward. It's an opportunity to take a higher road than tradition has carved, one that involves inner integrity rather than institutional sanctimony, one that involves minds and souls, not rules and roles, one that involves heart-based values beyond dollars and cents and the white picket fence. It's an opportunity to turn the rhetoric of goodness into real possibility. It's an opportunity to rethink family values and get clear about what it really takes to create happy homes, healthy souls, and well-adjusted children.

There is good news. Family values of real value can belong to anyone—gay or straight, liberal or conservative, religious or not. Bringing the best to bear in our families requires a commitment to personal development where emotions are regulated via mindful self-awareness. Then, empathic connection may be realized. Healthy family relations, whether it's between husband and wife or parent and child, involves acting with the kind of love that puts empathic feeling for others before ego-driven, knee-jerk emotional reactions and defenses. With mindful self-awareness, we can bring forth the best qualities in our nature.

In terms of shifting our culture's values and creating a more soulful society, we need to increase awareness of the problems at hand. Like any shift in our culture, whether it's going green, getting fit, or being smoke-free, the first step is to identify the negative influences and their effects, then bring this information to light. Cultural change begins with new stories being told and conversations taking hold, paving the way for progressive attitudes, values and behaviors to unfold.

Only by challenging the status quo can we change the status quo. We don't have to fall prey to advertising telling us what we need to buy in order to improve our lives. We don't have to mindlessly consume mass media, anymore than we have to mind-lessly consume junk food. It's time to take charge of the negative cultural influences raining down by stepping back and observing with perspective that which we are immersed in. Only then can we see that our culture's propagandized reality is not real, and the norms not normal.

Yes indeed, our culture has gone to hell in the proverbial hand basket. But the culprit is not a secular society, liberal values or the favorite scapegoat *de jour*, gay people. Like cancer cells run amok, capitalistic values have taken over the soul of our society. Consumerism and materialism have skewed our values with perverted notions of what really matters. In our all-consuming, outer-directed world, we have lost our inner lives where sound character dwells. We need don't need a to be warring against secularism or anything else with a culture war. This mentality is precisely the problem. We have enough war, violence, aggression and divisiveness in our culture. The solution lies in cultivating our humanity by enriching our lives emotionally and spiritually.

Let the evolution begin.

Afterword

I know there can be nothing more challenging than navigating the emotional currents of family life, and nothing more critical for sound family functioning. Because of this, the need for quality information to replace the rhetoric, myths and nostalgic ideals couldn't be greater. But the trials and tribulations of family life—what the challenges are, how to manage those challenges, and the personal growth needed for an optimally functioning family—are beyond the scope of this book, likely to be the topic of my next.

In the meantime, for those interested in personal development particularly as it applies to intimate and family life, I recommend visiting the website www.psychalive.org. This site provides a wealth of free information and affordable e-courses based on the work of Robert Firestone, Ph.D., whose astute and compassionate perspectives on parenting, family and intimate relations are transformative.

For more information and to receive my 10-point guideline for an emotionally healthy family life, please visit my website www.michelledeen.com.

Endnotes

1   Henderson, A. *"9 Reasons America Is a Lousy Place to Raise Kids."*
     Salon.com. 17 March 2016. N.p. Web. 6 Sept. 2016
2   Wilson, E.O. "The Biological Basis of Morality." *Atlantic Monthly.*
     April 1998. Web. 10 August 2016.
3   Firestone & Catlett. (2009). *The Ethics of Interpersonal Relationships.*
     London, U.K.: Karnac.
4   Ibid.
5   Firestone, R.W. (1997). *Combating Destructive Thought Processes:
     Separation Theory and Voice Therapy.* Santa Barbara, C.A.:
     The Glendon Association.
6   Firestone, R., Firestone, L., & Catlett, J. (2003). *Creating a Life of
     Meaning and Compassion: The wisdom of psychotherapy.* Washington,
     D.C.: American Psychological Association Books, Inc.
7   Olusoga, D. "The History of British Slave Ownership Has Been Buried:
     Now It's Scale Can Be revealed." *The Guardian.* 11 July 2015. n.p. Web.
     06 Sept. 2016.
8   Gabler, N. "Blowing the Biggest Political Story of the Last 50 Years."
     BillMoyers, 11 Mar. 2016. n.p. Web. 06 Sept. 2016.
9   Dean, J.W. (2006). *Conservatives Without Conscience.* New York, N.Y.:
     Viking Press. p. 18.
10   Ibid. p. 94.
11   Borba, M. (2001). *Building Moral Intelligence: The Seven Essential
     Virtues That Teach Kids to do the Right Thing.* San Francisco, C.A.:
     Jossey-Bass.
12   Altemeyer, B. (2006). *The Authoritarians.* Winnipeg, Canada:
     The Author. p. 140.
13   Ibid.
14   Ibid.

15 Ibid.

16 Eddy, Sherwood. (1941). *The Kingdom of God and the American Dream; the Religious and Secular Ideals of American History*. New York, N.Y.: Harper & Bros. Print. p. 6.

17 "The Responsibility of Citizens." *National Center for Constitutional Studies* n.p., n.d. Web. 06 Sept. 2016.

18 Sargent, G. "Brand Hillary." *The Nation*, 19 May 2005. n.p. Web. 30 June 2005.

19 *Progressive Policy Institute*. May 2005.

20 Celente, G. *Trends 2000: How to Prepare for and Profit from the Changes of the 21st Century*. New York, N.Y.: Warner Books, 1997. p. 213.

21 Dobson, J. "Focus on the Family: Helping Families Thrive." *Focus on the Family*. n.p., n.d. Web. 10 May 2005.

22 "What's the Big Deal About Gay Marriage?" *CitizenLink*. 16 March 2005. n.p. Web. 30 April 2005.

23 Cohn, D. "The States of Marriage and Divorce." *Pew Research Center*, Washington D.C. 15 October 2009. n.p. Web. 30 October 2009.

24 Stolberg, S.G. "Same Sex Marriage Amendment Fails in House." *New York Times*. n.p., 1 Oct. 2004. Web. 4 April 2006.

25 Coontz, Stephanie. (1992). *The Way We Never Were: American Families and the Nostalgia Trap*. New York, N.Y.: Basic.

26 Moore, T. (1992). *Care of the Soul: A Guide for Cultivating Depth and Sacredness in Everyday Life*. New York, N.Y.: HarperCollins. p. 73.

27 Coontz, S. (1992). *The Way We Never Were: American Families and The Nostalgia Trap*. New York, N.Y.; Basic.

28 Ibid.

29 Ibid.

30 Commission on National Goals. (1960). *Goals for Americans: The Report of the President's Commission on National Goals*. American Assembly, Columbia University. Englewood Cliffs, N.J.: Prentice-Hall. p. 259.

31 Schickel, R. "The Machine-Age Comic." *Time*. 3 August 2003. n.p. Web. 6 Sept. 2016.

32 Celente, G. (1997). *Trends 2000: How to Prepare for and Profit from the Changes of the 21st Century*. New York, N.Y.: Warner Books. p. 215.

33 Ibid.

34 *The Graduate*. Director, Mike Nichols. Producer, Lawrence Turman, 1967. Film.

35 Moore, T. (1992). *Care of the Soul: A Guide for Cultivating Depth and Sacredness in Everyday Life*. New York, N.Y.: HarperCollins. p. 5.

36   Coontz, S. (1992). *The Way We Never Were: American Families and The Nostalgia Trap.* New York, NY; BasicBooks. p. 39.

37   Ibid. p. 31.

38   Ibid. p. 286.

39   Ibid. p. 25.

40   Ibid. p. 36.

41   Friedan, Betty. (1963). *The Feminine Mystique.* New York: W.W. Norton.

42   "Values." *Webster's Encyclopedic Unabridged Dictionary: Of the English Language.* 1984. Print.

43   Ibid.

44   Covey, S. R. (1989). *The Seven Habits of Highly Effective People: Restoring the character ethic.* New York, N.Y.: Simon & Schuster. p. 35.

45   Beavers, W. Robert, et al. (1985). "The Beavers systems approach to family assessment." *Family Process,* Vol. 24:398-405.

46   Twitty, C., Lynn, L., & Moore, S. (1994). *The Conway Twitty Collection* [CD]. "That's My Job." MCA Records.

47   Rand, A. (1943). *The Fountainhead.* Indianapolis, I.N.: Bobbs-Merrill. p. 400.

48   Carrere, S., & Gottman, J.M. (1999). "Predicting Divorce among Newlyweds from the First Three Minutes of a Marital Conflict Discussion," *Family Process,* Vol. 38(3), 293-301.

49   Scarf, M. (1995). *Intimate Worlds.* New York, N.Y.: Random House. p. 36.

50   Bock, J., Harnick, S., & Stein, J. (1965). *Fiddler on the Roof.* New York, N.Y.: Crown.

51   Peck, M.S. (1978). *The Road Less Traveled: A New Psychology of Love, Traditional Values, and Spiritual Growth.* New York, N.Y.: Simon & Schuster.

52   *The Bible.* Galatians 5:22-23, Revised Standard Version, 1971.

53   Hite, Shere. (1995). *The Hite Report on the Family: Growing Up Under Patriarchy.* New York, N.Y.: Grove. p. 357.

54   Ibid.

55   Needleman, J., American Soul, Interview by C. Kjellberg. (2006, March 18). *It Takes a Village.*

56   Johns, A.C. (2013). *Cura Personalis: A course in medical miracles.* Place of publication not identified: Friesenpress. p. 303.

57   Bushman, B.J., Ridge, R.D., Das, E., & Busath, G.L. (2007, March 18). When God Sanctions Killing: Effect of Scriptural Violence on Aggression. *Psychological Science.* pp. 204-207.

58 Shakespeare, William. *The Merchant of Venice.* Ed. A. R. Braunmuller. New York, N.Y.: Penguin, 2000. (1.3.107).

59 Wolf, A.D. (2010). *Nurturing the Spirit: In Non-Sectarian Classrooms* Hollidaysburg, P.A.: Parent Children Press. pp. 14-15.

60 Hoffman, M.L. (2000). *Empathy and Moral Development: Implications for Caring and Justice.* Cambridge, U.K.: Cambridge University Press. p. 3.

61 Goleman, D. (1995). *Emotional Intelligence.* New York, N.Y.: Bantam Books. p. 108.

62 Ibid. p. xii.

63 Amen, D.G. (2002). *Healing the Hardware of the Soul: How Making the Brain-Soul Connection Can Optimize Your Life, Love, and Spiritual Growth.* New York, N.Y.: Free Press. p. 31.

64 LeDoux, J. E. (1996). *The Emotional Brain: The Mysterious Underpinnings of Emotional Life.* New York, N.Y.: Simon & Schuster.

65 Kanai, R., et.al. "Political Orientations Are Correlated with Brain Structure in Young Adults." *Current Biology,* 26 April 2011. n.p. Web. 20 May 2016.

66 Siegel, D. J. (1999). *The Developing Mind: Toward a Neurobiology of Interpersonal Experience.* New York, N.Y.: Guilford Press. p. 265.

67 Damasio, A. R. (1994). *Descartes' Error: Emotion, Reason, and the Human Brain.* New York, N.Y.: Putnam.

68 Blakeslee, S. "Humanity? Maybe It's in the Wiring." *New York Times.* 9 Dec. 2003 .n.p. Web. 3 April 2016.

69 Siegel, D. J. (1999). *The Developing Mind: Toward a Neurobiology of Interpersonal Experience.* New York, N.Y.: Guilford Press. p. 85.

70 Bowlby, J. (1988). *A Secure Base: Parent-child attachment and healthy human development.* New York, N.Y.: Basic Books.

71 Ainsworth, M. D. S. (1989). Attachments beyond infancy. *American Psychologist, 44,* 709-716.

72 Baumrind, D. (1989). Rearing Competent Children. In W. Damon (Ed). *Child Development Today and Tomorrow.* San Francisco, C.A.: Jossey-Bass. pp. 349-378.

73 Schore, Allan N. (1994). *Affect Regulation and The Origin of The Self: The Neurobiology of Emotional Development.* Hillsdale, N.J.: L. Erlbaum Associates. p. 45.

74 Ibid. p. 45.

75 Smith, M. B. "Humanistic Psychology." *Journal of Humanistic Psychology,* 43.4 (2003): 158.

76 Hoffman, M.L. (2000). *Empathy and Moral Development: Implications For Caring and Justice.* Cambridge, U.K.: Cambridge University Press. p. 22.

77 Robinson, J. (1994). Patterns of Development in Early Empathic Behavior. *Social Development, 3*(1), 125-145.

78 Rubin. (1998). Intrapersonal and Maternal Correlates of aggression, conflict and externalizing problems in toddlers. *Child Development, 69*(5), 1614-1629.

79 Sood, S., & Forehand, M. (2005). On self-referencing differences in judgment and choice. *Organizational Behavior and Human Decision Processes, 98*(2), 144-154.

80 Reynolds, S. J., & Ceranic, T. L. (2007). The effects of moral judgment and moral identity on moral behavior: An empirical examination of the moral individual. *Journal of Applied Psychology, 92*(6), 1610-1624.

81 Shengold, L. (1989) *Soul Murder: The Effects of Childhood Abuse and Deprivation.* New Haven, C.T.: Yale University Press.

82 Moore, T. (1992). *Care of the Soul: A guide for cultivating depth and sacredness in everyday life.* New York, N.Y.: HarperCollins. p. xviii.

83 Lama, Dalai. (1999). *Ethics for the New Millennium.* New York, N.Y.: Riverhead, Print. pp. 30-31.

84 Coles, R. (1997). *The Moral Intelligence of Children.* New York, N.Y.: Random House.

85 Ibid.

86 Ibid. p. 9.

87 Ibid. p. 170.

88 Morrison, K. (Director). "Bishop John Shelby Spong – The Church Invented Hell, It Does Not Exist." *Youtube.* 20 April 2014. n.p. Web. 12 August 2016.

89 Coles, R. (1997). *The Moral Intelligence of Children.* p. 178. New York, N.Y.: Random House.

90 Commission on National Goals. (1960). *Goals for Americans: The Report of the President's Commission on National Goals.* American Assembly, Columbia University. Englewood Cliffs, N.J.: Prentice-Hall. p. 1.

91 Lane, M. S. (2014). *Greek and Roman Political Ideas: An Introduction.* Gretna, LA.: Pelican Publishing, 2014.

92 Hamilton, C.V. "Why Did Jefferson Change 'Property' to the 'Pursuit of Happiness'?" *History News Network.* 27 January 2008. n.p. Web. 12 August 2016

93 Ibid.

94 Federer, B. "Only a virtuous people are capable of freedom." *World Net Daily.* 25 July 2015. n.p. Web. 17 August 2016.

95 Tocqueville, Alexis De. *Democracy in America.* London, U.K.: Penguin Classics, 2003. Print. p. 21.

96 Commission on National Goals. (1960). *Goals for Americans: The Report of the President's Commission on National Goals.* American Assembly, Columbia University. Englewood Cliffs, N.J.: Prentice-Hall. p. 55.

97 Tocqueville, Alexis de. (2003). *Democracy in America.* London, U.K.: Penguin Classics. p. 280.

98 Smith, A. (1976). *The Theory of Moral Sentiments.* Oxford, U.K.: Clarendon Press.

99 Gregoire, C. "Before 'The Wealth Of Nations,' Adam Smith Penned the Ultimate Guide to a Moral Life." *Huffington Post.* 9 Sept. 2014. n.p. Web. 12 August 2016.

100 Needleman, J. (2002). *The American Soul: Rediscovering the Wisdom of the Founders.* New York, N.Y.: J.P. Tarcher/Putnam. p. 23.

101 Ibid. p. 23.

102 Dill, K. "Report: CEOs Earn 330 Times Average Workers, 774 Times As Much As Minimum Wage Earners." *Forbes* 15 April 2014. n.p. Web. 12 August 2016.

103 Ibid.

104 Rand, A. (1962). "Conservatism: An Obituary." *Ayn Rand Institute.* n.p, n.d. Web. 12 August 2016.

105 Rand, A. (1982). *Philosophy, Who Needs It.* Indianapolis, I.N.: Bobbs-Merrill. p. 61.

106 Rand, A. (1966). *Capitalism, The Unknown Ideal.* New York, N.Y.: New American Library. p. 195.

107 Needleman, J. (2002). *The American Soul: Rediscovering the Wisdom of the Founders.* New York: J.P. Tarcher/Putnam. p 8.

108 Ibid. p. 155

109 King, M.L., Jr. (1957, August 11). *Conquering Self-Centeredness.* Speech presented in Dexter Avenue Baptist Church, Montgomery, Alabama.

110 Commission on National Goals. (1960). *Goals for Americans: The Report of the President's Commission on National Goals.* American Assembly, Columbia University. Englewood Cliffs, N.J.: Prentice-Hall. pp. 3-4.

111 Gingrich, N., & Haley, V. (2011). *A Nation Like No Other: Why American Exceptionalism Matters.* Washington, D.C.: Regnery Pub. p. 35.

112 Williams, K. "Promoting Marriage among Single Mothers: An Ineffective Weapon in the War on Poverty?" *Contemporary Families.org.* 6 January 2014. n.p. Web. 12 August 2016.

113 Coontz, S. (2016, March 31). "Americans Are Nostalgic for a Family Life That Never Existed." *Alternet.* 31 March 2016. n.p. Web. 12 August 2016.

114 Sanders, B. "On the Issues: Income and Wealth Inequality." *BernieSanders.com.* n.d., n.p. Web. 12 August 2016.

115 LaCapria, K. "643,000 Bankruptcies in the U.S. Every Year Due to Medical Bills." *Snopes.com.* 23 April 2016. n.p. Web. 12 August 2016.

116 McNamee, S. J., & Miller, R. K. (2004). *The Meritocracy Myth.* Lanham, M.D.: Rowman & Littlefield.

117 Brandeis, L. D. *Brandeis Legacy Fund for Social Justice,* Brandeis University. N.p., n.d. Web. 18 August 2016.

118 Commission on National Goals. (1960). *Goals for Americans: The Report of the President's Commission on National Goals.* American Assembly, Columbia University. Englewood Cliffs, N.J.: Prentice-Hall. pp. 44-45.

119 Rattner, S. "By Opposing Obama, the Republicans Created Trump." *New York Times. 13* April 2016. n.p. Web. 18 August 2016.

120 Commission on National Goals. (1960). *Goals for Americans: The Report of the President's Commission on National Goals.* American Assembly, Columbia University. Englewood Cliffs, N.J.: Prentice-Hall. p. 47.

121 Ibid.

122 Roosevelt, T. *Almanac of Theodore Roosevelt – 26th President of the U.S.A.* n.p., n.d. Web. 17 August 2016.

123 Lama, D. (1999). *Ethics for the New Millennium.* New York, N.Y.: Riverhead Books. p. 174.

124 Weeks, L. "When Did 'Kumbaya' Become Such A Bad Thing?" *National Public Radio.* 13 January 2012. n.p. Web. 18 August 2016.

125 Cooper, B., et. al. "Anxiety, Nostalgia, and Mistrust: Findings from the 2015 American Values Survey," *Public Religion Research Institute.* 17 Nov. 2015. n.p. Web. 18 August 2016.

126 Jefferson, Thomas, and Henry Augustine Washington. *The Writings of Thomas Jefferson: Inaugural Addresses and Messages. Replies to Public Addresses. Indian Addresses. Miscellaneous: 1. Notes on Virginia Paperback.* N.p.: Nabu, 2010.

127 Commission on National Goals. (1960). *Goals for Americans: The Report of the President's Commission on National Goals.* American Assembly, Columbia University. Englewood Cliffs, N.J.: Prentice-Hall. p. 6.

128 Ibid. p. 15.

129 Simon, C. "Marianne Williamson Brings Spirituality to Politics." *Harvard Gazette.* 13 October 2015. n.p. Web. 18 August 2016.
130 Williamson, M. Personal post. *Marianne Williamson Facebook Page.* 23 March 2016. n.p., Web. 18 August 2016.
131 Quote Retrieved from *Coolidge Foundation,* n.p., n.d. Web. 18 August 2016.
132 Lama, D. (2001). *Ethics for the New Millennium.* New York, N.Y.: Riverhead Books. pp. 16-17.
133 Ibid. p. 23.
134 Ibid. p. 22.
135 King, M.L., Jr. *"The Quest for Peace and Justice."* Lecture presented at Nobel Peace Prize 1964. *NobelPrize.org.* n.p., 11 Dec. 1964. Web. 18 August 2016.

CPSIA information can be obtained
at www.ICGtesting.com
Printed in the USA
FSOW01n1818130916
24940FS